BROKEN AND MENDED WITH CURSED BLOOD

BURUNDI, TRAPPED IN LIES, HATRED, CONSPIRACIES AND BLOOD STAINS - A WOUNDED NATION IN NEED OF HEALING

(A PETITION AND ADVOCACY)

Dr. Levi Rukundo Ph.D.

The Content

Preface

This book is a work dedicated to the *righting* of Burundi's war-torn history and serves as a petition and advocacy. A petition and advocacy that unveils genocide and many atrocities that tore the physical, psychological and social tissue of Burundians leaving a nation wounded and paralyzed. A petition and advocacy that corrects untruths spread across the world and taught to Burundi's citizens as their true past and a petition and advocacy that calls for efforts to support the healing of the nation. Many people have contributed to this informative work.

My experience as a diplomat at United Nations, participating in United Nations Security Councils, General Assemblies and other committee meetings has opened my eyes to lies, conspiracies and injustices that concern the world. My eye-opening experiences were the catalysis that propelled me to be a panel member at many conferences organized by universities and other platforms in the USA, in Canada, Europe and in Africa, on genocides and atrocities committed in the African Great Lakes Region.

Being born in Burundi, the heart of Africa, and having worked in intelligence service and in the office of the president during periods of the darkest time of Burundi's history, I discovered the agony and bitterness that this nation endured and continue to live today. I realized that our brothers and sisters need honest men and women to tell and to live for the truth. They need a "Moses" a "Gideon" and "Joshua" to get to the promise land, a nation in active healing and ultimately, a nation healed. It is for the healing of Burundi that I present this petition and advocacy to the United Nations, to the lawmakers of the United States of America, the European Union, Russia, China and of course, the Burundi Senate and Parliament because I realized that problems of Burundians are snares in which many societies of the world are trapped.

Each one of you can be an advocate of the nation of Burundi. The main cause, the root of evil that is affecting Burundi is from outside the country as outsiders come join forces with dormant demons in Burundi to produce deadly ideas of hatred and violence. Considering what is going on in the Great Lakes region of Africa in general, it is clear that some westerner powers that colonized Africa want to take by violence, the wealth of that region of Africa and everyone is aware of that reality. They create chaos by stirring up wars and maneuver travesty revolutions to position their allies in power. The Orientals as outsiders coming into Burundi also lust the African wealth, but they differ from westerners because they do not interfere with peace and stability of those Africans nations.   Affected Africans nations must become masterful of their destiny.

Those who stir up civil wars and use the maneuver of revolution are highly skilled to teleguide state coup. When those tools are at work, they simultaneously use the legal ground such as NGOs, human right reports and criminal courts to affect civil war.   For instance, seeing developers of UN reports, accepting to base their reports on one-sided opinion is a tangible sign that some reporters of UN so called experts, know conclusions before investigating. Knowing very well that no credible work can be based on a vision tainted by emotion and hatred.

In the case of 1972 unrecognized genocide against Hutu, you will see in detail with supporting proofs that Tutsi native of other regions other than Burundi, were also victims because they were assimilated to Hutu. There was a cruel plan to decimate not only intellectual citizens but also citizens literate at elementary level. This decimation was not based on the victims being able to organize conspiracy against the government or leave writings on the committed atrocities for the future generations, but it was a "killing of gene pool", those able to learn, study and think intellectually. It was done with the aim to prove the existence of the supremacy of Tutsi ethnic group over others ethnic groups, with the organizers of the selective genocide knowing that intellectual ability is largely hereditary. The genetic hecatomb and barbarian acts were perfectly committed, and communities are today in agony and are suffering from those marks harrow.

European countries that are intensely interested in the Great Lakes region of Africa today know very well that there was genocide in Burundi. They allowed the perpetrators to quietly complete their macabre task and have sufficient time to erase the traces of their crimes and to be able to control the narrative and the speeches on the national and international level because they were emboldened by the silent acquiescence of their western masters. That was the explicit tactic employed to allow a minority group to commit a perfect crime during a period of time when the involvement of those countries gave the appearance of work being done to solve the dilemma of the killings. This tactic was practiced to protect power and those who killed to conquer the power by sacrificing victims, orphans and survivors of all blind barbarism. But it is time that the world wakes up to stand and truthfully and rightfully advocate for all vulnerable human being.

I have a deep love for a better world for every human kind. I respect every nation and cherish the human right of everyone. This is my position and the reason I spread the truth, no matter the coast.

INTRODUCTION

Every nation has its own history of struggles, with a past filled with revolutions, killings and cases of betrayal, murder and sometimes mass atrocities. When it comes to the region of the Great Lakes of Africa and the kingdoms around, the past shows masses of bloodshed and cyclic massacres. The truth on all those human rights violations has been purposely blurred and we need to understand why the truth is distorted. Burundi being one of the small countries of that region, its nation carries severe wounds that need to be mended. Unfortunately, the diagnosis of the evil of Burundi is wrongly established through different opinions. The international community fails to understand the origin of the political sickness of the country, and consequently, their efforts have been largely in vain.

The nation of Burundi abounds with criminals and their victims, and with no justice or reconciliation in its history. Instead there are actions to cover-up the crimes committed, including the crime of genocide. Where is the country heading? That is the question of those who are truly concerned for Burundi. Decedents of those who lost parents and relatives carry deep wounds that need attention. These whose parents and relatives were killed are not spared from shame, guilt, condemnation and embarrassment. This causes distress to everyone in the country. Individuals of both groups, the killers and survivors of those killed present mental and social disorders that need urgent collective therapies. Burundi has been in the world's spotlight for a very long time for genocide and other atrocious crimes committed there, but very little has been done to foster sustainable peace and healing in the country. The time of lies, hypocrisy and conspiracy must come to an end.

The attempts of the international community to solve the country's problems were superficial at best, and sometimes unnecessary measures were taken that ultimately worsened the situations. The Burundian-evil is deeply rooted into the unrecognized 1972 genocide, along with other atrocities that have led to unsolved conflicts and twisted facts. Imagine a nation that underwent the tragedy of mysteriously losing 1/10 of its population in one ethnic group. With the killings being essentially done against educated individuals, military officers, professors, teachers, students, religious leaders and business men all leaving behind orphans and widows, and still no justice had ever been done. A country that lost two Hutu presidents in less than one year, in October 1993 and April 1994 and once again hit by the waves of killings of members of the government, members of parliament, governors, priests, pastors, and many more intellectual and less educated and poorer citizens. It seems that people overlook the impact of those tragedies in the collective thoughts of the nation. The history of the country must be corrected to tell our truths.

When the international community, including the United Nations, intervenes, it establishes a misinformed, misguided and corrupted solutions of the situation based on a one-sided opinion. For instance, instead of considering the situation globally, they attempt to use the International Criminal Court against children of the victims, leaving behind criminals. Such situations result in things become more complicated. In such context, people see conspiracy, manipulation by the International community and cause some Burundians to become viciously hypocritical, dishonest, sadistic and deceitful. The nation presents with wounds, scars and symptoms of severe mental disorder and a strategic and sustainable collective therapy is needed to address these problems.

Several questions about what is truly happening in and to Burundi have to be answered officially. Contrary to the false answers and lies that are spread across the internet. Burundians need to know the truth about what happened in 1965, 1969, 1972, 1988, 1993... Unanswered questions may plunge the country into more and more crisis and violence that will continue to take many more lives of innocent people, as we know for sure from the atrocities committed in 1969, 1972, 1988, 1991, 1993, that were a logical continuation of the unnamed mass killing of 1965.

The country knows the phenomenon such regionalism, clannism, injustice and social inequality, as well as tolerance in the use of drugs and other substances, a high rate of mental disorders, denial of self-social identity, excessive spiritualism, aimless wandering of some groups and a visceral hatred between Hutu and Tutsi. These conditions will surely lead the country to another tragedy if nothing is done.

This petition-advocacy outlines pertinent details of the 1972 genocide, description of atrocities endured by survivors and victim's family members, along with proposed solution to restore the Nation of Burundi. The nation was broken and "mended" with cursed blood, hatred, lies and conspiracy.

CHAP I OVERVIEW OF MAIN EVENTS

Allow us to take you to the darkest time of the true history of Burundi. This will make you have more compassion and pity that lead to an advocacy for the wounded nation. For a better understanding of the evil root of the Burundian evil and realize how superficial is the effort of the international community at the occurrence, the united nations, please read carefully the chronology of main events that occurred in Burundi since 1890 to 2017 and compare those paramount events to what is called the effort of the United Nations to solve the Burundi problems.

A. Chronology of main events in Burundi since 1890 to 2017 and attempts of the United Nations

-1890   A conference in Brussels gave Rwanda and Burundi to the German Empire as colonial spheres of interest in exchange for renouncing all claims on Uganda.
-1901   Feb 23, Britain and Germany agreed on a boundary between German East Africa [later Tanganyika,

Rwanda and Burundi] and Nyasaland [later Malawi].
-1919: Germany lost Ruanda-Urundi to Belgium under the League of Nations mandate system. Both Germany and Belgium ruled through the traditional system of Tutsi nobles, headed by the Mwami.

-1950s: (Burundi) Tutsi prince Louis Rwagasore founded a multi-ethnic party, the Union for National Progress (UPRONA)

B. Independence

-1962: Rwanda and Burundi became independent from Belgium as separate countries, even though both were ethnically and culturally united. Burundi's first post-independence government was controlled by Tutsi while the first Rwandan government was Hutu.

-1965: Multi-ethnic government broke down during the first elections after Hutu politicians won control of both houses of parliament. King Mwambutsa abolished the legislature before it could meet and the (Hutu-dominated) army revolted. The army coup was crushed by Tutsi officers led by Michel Micombero. King Mwambutsa IV fled the country and his son Ntare V assumed power. Micombero dismissed Ntare and authorized reprisals that resulted in about 5,000 Hutu deaths. Micombero set up a "Government of Public Safety" modeled after the French revolutionary government that included extraordinary police powers for a strong, centralized government.

-1969: There was a major purge of Hutu elite.

-1972: Uganda's Idi Amin assisted Micombero to arrest NtareV (who later died while in custody in Burundi). Citing riots that killed 2000 top Tutsi officials, Micombero declared martial law. Educated Hutu were targeted and between 80,000 and 500,000 died, while more than 100,000 Hutu fled to neighboring countries and did not return. Meanwhile, France, China and Libya increased their military aid to the Burundi government, and a report by the International Commission of Jurists and the International League of the Rights of Man identified systematic human rights abuses by the government against Hutu citizens.

-1974: Micombero revised the constitution to create a one-party state under UPRONA.

-1975: Although the UN Commission on Human Rights opened prosecution against Burundi officials for human rights violations against Hutu citizens, the case later was dropped.

-1976: Micombero was overthrown by a military coup led by Colonel Jean-Baptiste Bagaza, but power remained in the hands of a Tutsi elite composed of army, civil servants and UPRONA.

-1985: (Burundi) Bagaza widened repression against opponents of the government to include the Catholic Church.

-1987: Bagaza was overthrown by Pierre Buyoyo in another military coup.

-1988: There was more ethnic violence in Burundi when the army killed 5-25,000 Hutu in reprisal for Hutu murders of several Tutsi in the north. Roughly 60,000 Hutu fled to Rwanda and another 100,000 became homeless in Burundi.

-1991: The Revolutionary Party for the Liberation of the Hutu People (PALIPEHUTU) launched further attacks, starting a new round of violence.

-1991: Buyoyo increased Hutu participation in government. Although Hutus dominate ministerial posts, final power rested with the the all-Tutsi Military Committee of National Salavation.

-1992: A new constitution opened the way for multi-party elections.

-1993   Jun, Melchior Ndadaye was elected president in the first democratic election in Burundi.

-1993   Oct 21, Burundi's first Hutu president, Melchior Ndadaye, was assassinated by Tutsi soldiers. 5 soldiers were sentenced to death for the murder then released. The military coup caused 525,000 Hutu's to flee. Civil war followed and over the next dozen years some 300,000 people, mostly civilians, were killed.

-1994   Apr 6, the presidents of Rwanda and Burundi Cyprian Ntaryamira, president of Burundi (1993-94) were killed on a return trip from Tanzania in a shot down plane in   Kigali,   Rwanda;

-1994   President Sylvestre Ntibantunganya took office in   Burundi.

-1996   Jan, The Burundi president warned that the

country may be on the brink of a possible collapse due to fighting between the ethnic fanatics in the Hutu majority and the Tutsi-dominated army.
-1996   Jan, Tutsi militants closed down the Burundi capital in a general strike. They accused the president of backing massacres by Hutus after the killing of a predecessor in 1993.
-1996   Apr, the Red Cross said more than 55,000 people have been driven from their homes by ethnic fighting that intensified last month. More than 100,000 have been killed since 1993 in the conflict between majority Hutus and minority Tutsis. The fighting occurred in the capital city of Bujumbura. 235 civilians died when the Burundi army attacked villages at Buhoro.
-1996   May 3, A handwritten account reached the Burundi capital that described the massacre of 375 people at the Kivyuka village market by government soldiers angry over recent rebel attacks on local power line towers. An army spokesman denied the charges.
-1996   May 16, Sylvestre Ntibantunganya, the Burundi's Hutu president, has called his army "paralyzed and useless" and given it a week to stop ethnic violence between Tutsi armed forces and Hutu rebels.
-1996   May 30, Suspected Hutu rebels of the Council for the Defense of Democracy killed at least 61 and wounded 25 Tutsis in eastern Burundi.

-1996   Jun 4, In Burundi 3 Swiss Red Cross workers were ambushed and killed while delivering supplies near the village of Mugina. The Tutsi-dominated Uprona Party denied any role and said the killings were the work of

gangs of the Coalition for the Defense of Democracy, the main Hutu rebel group.
-1996   Jun 13, A Burundi army report claimed that 50 Hutu rebels were killed in an attack on a training camp.
-1996   Jul 4, Unidentified gunmen killed 80 people in an attack on a tea factory 15 miles northeast of Bujumbura, Burundi.
-1996   Jul 21, In Burundi Hutu rebels killed 320 Tutsis, mostly women and children, at a refugee camp 45 miles north of the capital.
-1996   Jul 25, In Burundi the military seized power and named former president Pierre Buyoya, a Tutsi, as president. Hutu officials sought refuge in foreign embassies. Burundian Hutus fled to Zaire's South Kivu province, base of the National Council for the Defense of Democracy, an extremist Burundi Hutu movement backed by Zaire.
-1996   Jul 26, UN sources said that 268 Hutu civilians were killed in Burundi's Gitega province. The Tutsi army said Hutu rebels attacked a coffee factory in Giheta.
-1996   Jul 27, In Burundi a Tutsi-led army killed at least 30 Hutu in retaliation for an attack on a coffee plantation. Villagers said Tutsi soldiers massacred about 1,000 Hutus as they roamed from village to village in Gitega province.
-1996   Aug 13, the last 2 commercial flights left Burundi as the outside world tightened sanctions to punish the new military regime.
-1996   Aug 20, In Burundi Pierre Buyoya sacked his army chief, Jean Bikomagu, who was implicated in the 1993 assassination of the first Hutu president Melchior Ndadaye.

-1996   Aug 27, The last Rwandan refugee camp in Burundi   closed.
-1996   Aug, After the Burundi coup of Jul 25, former Tanzanian President Julius Nyerere led East African leaders to impose sanctions on Burundi and force Buyoya to restore   democratic   rule.
-1996   Sep 3, Hutu guerrillas attacked an army garrison and local government headquarters in northern Burundi.
-1996   Oct 21, In Murambi village, Burundi, some 300 (258-435) Hutu refugees returned from Zaire and were killed as they sought refuge in a village church.
-1997   Jan 5, In Burundi the Tutsi-led army attacked and killed hundreds of Hutus in a dispute over land at Bukeye in central Burundi.

-1997   Jan 11, Soldiers shot and killed 126 Burundian Hutu refugees trying to break out of a holding camp in the northeast. Seven soldiers were arrested for the slayings then   released.
-1997   Feb 21, It was reported that Burundi troops killed more than 150 civilians in reprisals for rebel attacks. 100 people were killed at Mugara and fifty near Maramvya.
-1997   Apr 16, African leaders of 7 nations eased their embargo on Burundi to alleviate local suffering.
-1997   May 29, It was reported that the Tutsi-led army killed more than 40 Hutu rebels that included Hutu students kicked out of Bujumbura University in 1995.
-1997   Aug 1, A UN report from this day was made public in 2000 and cited Tutsi informants claiming that they helped to shoot down the airplane carrying Rwandan Pres. Juvanal Habyarimana on Apr 6, 1994.

-1997   Oct 20, Soldiers of the Tutsi army packed 40 civilians into a rural school in the region of Kibezi and tossed a grenade inside. All were killed. Major Andre Nijongabo, a Burundi army commander, defended the incident claiming that the dead were "genocidal terrorists." Hutu rebels had burned 18 schools a week ago.
-1998   Jan 1, some 1-2 thousand Hutu rebels attacked a Burundi military base and near the main airport and 150 civilians, 30 rebels and 2 soldiers were reported killed. Later reports said as many as 300 were killed and that the army had sealed up the area.
-1998   Jan 12, In Burundi Hutu rebels attacked army positions and at least 55 people were killed.
-1988   Jan 21, In Burundi Hutu rebels killed 45 people in 2 attacks, and 20 rebels died in a subsequent battle with the army.
-1998   Jan 28, Burundi Colonel Firmin Sinzoyiheba, the Tutsi minister of defense, was killed in a helicopter crash in the Gihinga Hills.
-1998   Burundi military leader Pierre Buyoya was sworn in as president by the democratically elected parliament.
-1998   Oct 28, In Burundi 34 people were killed south of the capital.
-1999   Jan 19, Rebels based in Tanzania killed 59 civilians in Makamba, Burundi and in Muresi Hill 76 civilians were killed.
-1999   Jan 28, In Burundi officials reported that at least 178 civilians had been killed over the last 2 weeks in clashes between rebels and government troops.
-1999   Aug 29, In Burundi Hutu militiamen attacked 2 neighborhoods outside Bujumbura and killed at least 26

civilians.

-1999	Sep 24, In Burundi the government reported that Hutu rebels had hacked to death 11 civilians in 2 separate attacks.

-1999	Sep 26, in Nyambuye, Burundi, 30 people were killed in a Catholic church. Unidentified men in uniform opened fire while mostly Hutu worshipers prayed.

-1999	Sep 28, It was reported that the Burundi army has recently forced over 200,000 villagers into makeshift camps without food or water and that 100 people had died over the past week.

-1999	Oct 12, In Burundi Hutu rebels attacked a UN humanitarian convoy and killed 9 people at the Muzye refugee camp in Rutana.

-1999	Nov 22, In Tanzania it was reported that some 500 people per day were fleeing into the country from Burundi as fighting in Burundi intensified.

-1999	Dec 1, African leaders chose Nelson Mandela as the new mediator for talks on ending the 6-year civil war in Burundi.

-1999	Dec 20, In Burundi Gabriel Gisabwamana, a Hutu member of parliament, was shot and killed by soldiers at a checkpoint.

-1999	Dec 31, Burundian soldiers killed at least 43 people including children in the Kabezi commune in Bujumbura Rural province.

-2000	Jan 16, Nelson Mandela addressed peace talks in Arusha, Tanzania, and admonished the leaders of Burundi for having failed their people and all of Africa.

-2000	Feb 21, In Tanzania African presidents and

European ministers appealed to Burundi's leaders to negotiate a swift end to the civil war.
2000   Mar 3, In Burundi the authorities under int'l. pressure began dismantling 6 of nearly 60 camps holding hundreds of thousands of Hutu civilians.
-2000   Apr 25, In Burundi 66 people were reported killed in renewed fighting between Hutu rebels and government   troops.
-2000   Jun 7, Burundi President Pierre Buyoya made concessions to end the 7-year war. He agreed to integrate the Tutsi-led army and to close down the regroupment camps by July 31.
-2000   Jul 7, The East African Community (EAC), founded in 1967, was resurrected following its collapse in 1977. The regional club included six members: Burundi, Kenya, Rwanda, South Sudan, Tanzania, and Uganda. In 2005 members agreed on a customs union and in 2010 they agreed on a common market.
-2000   Jul 22, In Burundi uniformed men killed 53 men, women and children in the village of Butaganzwa, when they refused to go to a government regroupment camp.
-2000   Aug 6, In Burundi Hutu rebels ambushed a truck carrying military cadets and 28 soldiers and 6 civilians were killed near Nyabiraba village.
-2000   Aug 28, Pres. Clinton stopped in Burundi where Tutsi minority parties refused to sign a deal with the Hutu majority. Clinton urged the parties to work for peace.
-2000   Dec 28, Hutu rebels ambushed a commuter bus outside Bujumbura and killed 20 passengers.
-2001   Apr 9, In Burundi villagers were caught in crossfire fighting between the army and Hutu rebels. 11-30

people were killed and thousands were forced to flee their   homes.
-2001   Apr 18, The Burundi army put down a coup attempt by junior officers opposed to Pres. Buyoya's negotiations   with   Hutu   rebels.
-2001   Jun 3, It was reported the Burundi was poised for war due to conflicts between the Hutu majority and Tutsi minority.
-2001   Jul 23, In Burundi Pres. Buyoya survived a coup attempt by Tutsi soldiers and sealed a power-sharing accord with Hutu politicians. The Arusha accord called for Buyoya to lead for 18 months followed by a Hutu president for another 18 months with elections to follow.
-2001   Sep 28, It was reported that clashed in Burundi between government forces and Hutu rebels had killed at least 19 civilians and 22 soldiers over the last week.
-2001   Oct, Some 150 political exiles returned to participate in the 3-year transition to democracy. Some 700 South African soldiers massed in Bujumbura to help protect   the   exiles.
-2001   Nov 6, In Munini, Burundi, 24 civilians were reported dead from fighting between Hutu rebels and the Tutsi   dominated   army.
-2001   Nov 9, Hutu rebels in Burundi abducted 80 teenage boys and 4 teachers from 3 schools in Ruyigi. Forced recruitment was believed to be the reason. Hundreds of youths escaped and at least 3 were left dead.
-2001   Dec 7, Int'l. donors promised Burundi over $760 million for reconstruction and to fight AIDS. About 11.3% of the   population   was   infected   with   HIV.

-2001   Dec 25, Burundi Maj. Gen. Gahiro reported that 515 Hutu rebels and 28 soldiers had been killed in the Tenga region since Nov 26. He said fighting the area was liberated   but   that   fighting   continued.
-2002   Jan 15, fighting began in Burundi between the army and Hutu rebels. At least 60 people were dead after a   week.
-2002   Mar 19, In Burundi fighting between the Tutsi dominated army and Hutu rebels forced over 16,000 people from their homes over the last 2 days.
-2002   Jun 4, National Liberation Forces rebels, one of 2 rebel Hutu groups, attacked military positions near Bujumbura and caused thousands of people to flee the area.
-2002   Jun 11, More than 40 Burundian refugees returning home from Tanzania after years in exile died when the truck carrying them overturned, an official said.
-2002   Jun 21, In Burundi a court has sentenced 11 people to death and 16 others to life imprisonment for taking part in massacres that followed the 1993 assassination of Burundi's first democratically elected leader.
-2002   Jun 27, Burundian rebels said they had repelled a major government offensive against bases in the Kibira National Park, saying 35 government soldiers had been killed   in   five   day   of   fighting.
-2002   Jul 26, The Burundian army claimed it has killed at least 500 Hutu rebels during fighting over the last two weeks,   while   suffering   only   15   losses.
-2002   Aug 30, In Burundi the army reportedly killed 48 Hutu   rebels   in   clashes   outside   Bujumbura.

-2002		Sep 9, In Burundi 183 civilians were killed by uniformed men in an area of heavy fighting between government troops and rebels. On Sep 18 the government promised an investigation.
-2002		Oct 7, In Burundi 2 smaller factions of the main rebel movements signed a cease-fire aimed at ending the 9-year civil war.
-2002		Nov 2, In Burundi at least 15,000 people have fled their homes as fighting between the army and rebels escalated despite peace talks.
-2002		Nov 22, Burundi's largest rebel faction launched a mortar attack on Bujumbura from the surrounding hills, causing thousands of residents to flee their homes in the northern part of the city.
-2002		Dec 3, In Burundi Pres. Pierre Buyoya and Pierre Nkurunziza, leader of the main faction of the Forces for the Defense of Democracy, or FDD, agreed to a cease-fire in their 9-year civil war (effective Dec 30), in theory leaving only one rebel group fighting in a conflict that has killed more than 200,000 people.
-2003		Jan 15, In Burundi 2 weeks of fighting between the Tutsi-dominated army and two rebel groups has displaced more than 30,000 people in two provinces.
-2003		Mar 22, Burundi's hardline Hutu rebel group expressed satisfaction with its first round of peace talks in Switzerland.
-2003		Mar 26, The Burundian army attacked a rebel stronghold in a Kibira forest with mortars and artillery, killing 68 insurgents. Rebels said only 2 fighters were killed.
-2003		Apr 2, Burundi said Ethiopia, Mozambique and South Africa will send 3,500 peacekeepers to enforce a

truce ending nearly 10 years of civil war.
-2003   Apr 8, In Burundi battles started between the Tutsi-dominated army and the rebel Forces for the Defense of Democracy, or FDD, after the army tried to intercept insurgents moving into Gitega province. More than 6,000 people fled their homes in response.
-2003   Apr 19, In Burundi a mortar shell apparently fired from rebel positions in the hills northwest of Bujumbura crashed into a house, killing three children and wounding a woman and another child. The latest fighting has forced 50,000 people to flee their homes.
-2003   Apr 30, Burundi's Tutsi minority handed over the presidency to Domitien Ndayizeye of the Hutu majority as part of the peace process aimed at ending 9 1/2 years of civil war.
-2003   May 11, The Burundi army killed 23 Hutu rebels during fighting in central Burundi, but the insurgents claimed the dead were civilians.
-2003   Jul 8, In Burundi Hutu rebels fought their way into part of the capital, trading gun, mortar and grenade fire with the Tutsi-dominated army. Thousands fled their homes.
-2003   Jul 10, In Burundi recent fighting left an estimated 170 people killed according to a UN estimate. 6,000 to 7,000 others had been forced to flee their homes.
-2003   Sep 21, The latest outbreak of fighting between Hutu rebels and the army in Burundi's decade-long civil war has killed at least 12 people on the outskirts of Bujumbura.
-2003   Oct 27, In Burundi fighting between government soldiers and Hutu rebels has forced more than 5,000

people to flee their homes in the hills surrounding the capital of Bujumbura.
-2003   Nov 2, Burundi's president and main rebel leader signed a peace agreement, but efforts to end the decade-long civil war were threatened by renewed fighting between Tutsi-dominated government troops and other Hutu rebels.
-2003   Nov 10, In Burundi Hutu rebels bombarded the capital with rockets, killing 5 people, destroying part of the Chinese Embassy and striking the home of a U.S. military attaché.
-2003   Nov 16, Burundi's government signed a comprehensive power-sharing plan with the Hutu FDD, country's largest rebel group, a major step toward ending a 10-year war that has killed at least 200,000 people.
-2003   Nov 19, Rebel holdouts in Burundi clashed with government troops in a capital slum, killing 11 people, mainly noncombatants caught in the crossfire.
-2003   Dec 22, An international human rights group criticized a peace agreement giving soldiers and rebels temporary immunity from prosecution for atrocities committed against civilians in Burundi's 10-year civil war.
-2003   Dec 29, In Burundi gunmen killed Monsignor Michael Courtney, the pope's ambassador, firing on his car as he was returning from a funeral.
-2003   Dec, In Burundi the Forces for the Defense of Democracy (FDD), the biggest Hutu rebel group, joined Burundi's transitional government. FNL rebels under Agathon Rwasa (39) continued to lob mortar shells into Bujumbura.
-2004   Jan 12, In Burundi Hutu rebels killed 17 people,

including five soldiers, in attacks northwest of Bujumbura over the last 2 days.
2004 Feb 24, An earthquake shook Burundi, killing three people and destroying at least two dozen homes.
-2004 Aug 13, The FNL, a Burundian Hutu rebel faction, raided Gatumba camp, a UN refugee camp in western Burundi, shooting and hacking to death 160 people. The camp sheltered Congolese ethnic Tutsi refugees, known as the Banyamulenge.
-2004 Burundi created a national army out of former army and seven former rebel movements.
-2005 Feb 28, Burundians voted on a new constitution that enshrines Hutu control by allotting them 60% of parliamentary seats with 40% for Tutsis.
-2005 Jun 13, Burundi began forced repatriation of thousands of Rwandan refugees, who feared reprisals at home. The UN condemned the action.
-2005 Jul 4, Burundi's main Hutu ex-rebel group, the Forces for the Defense of Democracy (FDD), won a comfortable victory in legislative elections, taking 58.23% of the vote.
-2005 Aug 19, Pierre Nkurunziza (40), a former Hutu rebel leader, was chosen by lawmakers as Burundi's president, culminating an internationally mediated effort that hopes to bring peace to a central African nation wrecked by a dozen years of ethnic war. Burundi's 12-year civil war left as many as 300,000 people dead.
-2005 Dec 31, A first group of UN peacekeepers from Mozambique left Burundi as part of a phased withdrawal of troops that will end in December next year.
-2006 Feb 27, In Burundi a government official

acknowledged that rogue soldiers and police officers have executed and tortured suspected rebels and civilians.

-2006	May 29, Burundi's only hold-out rebel group began talks with the government in an effort to end the central African country's 12-year civil war.

-2006	Jun 17, Burundi's President Pierre Nkurunziza left to sign a cease-fire agreement with the country's last rebel group in neighboring Tanzania as his government works toward ending a 12-year conflict.

-2006	Jun 30, The UN Security Council voted unanimously to conclude its peacekeeping mission in Burundi on Dec. 31 and replace it with a UN office to help promote development and democracy in the central African nation.

2006	Aug 6, In Burundi gunmen hurled a grenade at a bar frequented by army officers, killing four people. Authorities said the attack was an attempt to undermine the government.

-2006	Aug 21, Burundi police arrested former President Domitien Ndayizeye, apparently in connection with an alleged plot to overthrow the tiny central African country's government.

-2006	Sep 5, Burundi Vice-President Alice Nzomukunda resigned over corruption and human rights abuses that she says are hampering her nation's progress.

-2006	Sep 7, Burundi's government and the country's last rebel group, the National Liberation Forces (FNL) signed a permanent cease-fire as the central African nation emerges from 12 years of civil war.

-2006	Oct 17, The United States said it plans to take in

about 10,000 Burundian refugees from Tanzania, many of whom fled their landlocked nation as far back as 1972.
-2006   Oct 25, A rights group said Burundi's spy agency has executed 38 people and arbitrarily detained 200 others since the Central African nation's new government came to power. New York-based Human Rights Watch accused President Pierre Nkurunziza's year-old government of failing to prosecute those accused of extra-judicial   killings.
-2007   Mar 15, Human Rights Watch released a report that said Children in Burundi suffer serious abuses in prison, including torture, rape and food shortages, in a criminal justice   system   that   treats   them   as   adults.
-2007   Apr 18, Burundi, Rwanda, the Democratic Republic of Congo and Uganda adopted a joint military strategy to fight rebel groups operating in the war-scarred Great   Lakes   region.
-2007   May 18, A group of 88 Burundians who have lived as refugees in neighboring Tanzania for up to 35 years became the first of some 8,500 to head to the US for a   new   life.
-2007   May 23, The UN human rights commissioner said that Burundi has agreed to set up a tribunal to try people suspected of genocide and war crimes during its 12-year civil   war.
-2007   May 25, In Burundi 61 countries and international organizations promised 656 million dollars (488 million euros) during a donors' roundtable in the capital Bujumbura. The World Bank considers Burundi, where 70% of the population lives below the poverty line, the world's third-poorest   nation.

-2007   Jul 21, Jean Berchmans Ndayishimiye, the military leader of Burundi's last rebel group (FNL), escaped back to the bush, sparking fears of renewed civil conflict.
-2007 Aug 19, Simultaneous grenade attacks were launched on the homes of five Burundian politicians who recently criticized the president, injuring three but failing to harm the targets.
-2008   Mar 14, Five Burundi insurgents and a government soldier were killed in a clash with the army in the north of the war-wracked central African country's capital.
-2008   Apr 17, In Burundi suspected rebels attacked the capital, Bujumbura. A series of attacks killed at least 17 people.
-2008   May 18, In Burundi as the government and rebels sought unsuccessfully to reach agreement in negotiations to reinstate a 2006 ceasefire deal, the army attacked National Liberation Forces (FNL) rebel positions south of Bujumbura.
-2008   May 25, Burundian officials said the army killed three rebels near the capital over the weekend, the latest in a series of violent clashes in the central African nation.
-2008   May 26, Burundi's government and last active rebel group signed an unconditional ceasefire agreement, raising hopes of a definitive end to the small central African nation's 15-year civil war.
-2008   Jun 8, Burundi's top rebel leader and the government's chief negotiator pledged to work to end 15 years of civil war as they arrived in South Africa for talks on the country's peace process.
-2008   Oct 16, Around one million Burundian children

under the age of five suffer chronic malnutrition, the UN food agency announced as it marked World Food Day in the tiny central African nation.
-2008   Nov 22, Burundi's parliament adopted a new set of laws abolishing the death penalty for the first time in the troubled central African country.
-2009   Jan 2, In Burundi an 8-year-old albino boy was hacked to death in front of his mother and made off with his arms and legs. The body parts of a single albino, to be used in witch doctor potions, fetched about $1000. This attack followed another on a 6-year-old girl.
-2009   Mar 13, In Burundi an albino man was murdered and dismembered overnight by suspected smugglers with links to Tanzanian witch doctors, the fourth such case in a month in the central African nation.
-2009   Dec 30, In Burundi the last South African soldiers from the African Union Special Task Force still operating in Burundi completed their mission and left the country for good to return to South Africa.
-2010   May 3, In Burundi attackers chopped off the limbs of a 5-year-old albino boy and pulled out his mother's eye, killing them over the belief that their body parts would bring wealth and success. Ten assailants armed with guns and grenades killed Desire Vyegura (5) and his mother, Susann Vyegura. Thoma Vyegura, who was not albino, was also killed while trying to protect his daughter and grandson.
-2010   Jun 1, In Burundi 5 presidential candidates in upcoming elections said they're withdrawing from the race because of rigged voting. The candidates announced their withdrawal following a May 24 vote that

opposition parties said were rigged by the ruling party, which received 64 percent of votes. Four rounds of voting remain.

-2010   Jun 4, Burundi's main Tutsi party followed five opposition parties in pulling out from the central African nation's June presidential poll, leaving serving leader Pierre Nkurunziza as the sole candidate.

-2010   Jun 21, In Burundi the president of the ruling party's youth league was assassinated by unknown gunmen.

-2010   Jun 22, In Burundi 2 people were reported killed and several wounded overnight in the latest spate of attacks to rock the East African nation amid a tense electoral   crisis.

-2010   Jun 27, Burundi's police overnight arrested six senior officials from an opposition party, as the troubled central African nation prepared for a controversial presidential   election.

-2010   Jun 28, Burundi began voting for a president. Incumbent President Pierre Nkurunziza was the lone candidate.

-2010   Jun 30, In Burundi politicians boycotting the elections dismissed the results as a sham.

-2010   Jul 2, it was reported that grenade attacks in Burundi have killed 8 people and wounded almost 50 over   the   last   month.

-2010   Jul 22, Burundi was labeled as the most corrupt country in East Africa in a survey by Transparency International. Rwanda was found to be the least corrupt among the five countries in the region.

-2010   Sep 24, Agathon Rwasa, a former rebel chief in

Burundi, appealed by letter to UN chief Ban Ki-moon to intervene and prevent the east African nation from falling again into violent conflict. Rwasa headed the ex-rebel National Liberation Forces, which became a political party in 2009 after a peace deal ended Burundi's 13-year civil war.
-2011   Jul 1, Burundi's President Pierre Nkurunziza appealed for the first time to opposition leaders in exile to return home and begin a dialogue, in a speech to mark the country's independence.
-2011   Jul 4, In Burundi an armed gang raided two police posts in Bujumbura and dropped leaflets saying they were members of a rebel group called FRONABU-Tabara (Burundi National Front). Four suspects were arrested.
-2011   Jul 19, In Burundi at least nine people died in clashes between unidentified "armed gangsters" and security forces in northwest Cibitoke province. Two soldiers, a police officer and six "gangsters" were among the dead.
-2011   Aug 11, Burundi and South Africa signed several cooperation deals including in defense, education and agriculture during President Zuma's visit to the central African country.
-2011   Sep 16, Burundi opposition leader Agathon Rwasa, suspected to be behind a spate of violent incidents, accused state security forces of massacring and torturing his supporters.
-2011   Sep 18, In Burundi armed men burst into a pub in Gatumba. One wounded man said an attacker yelled: "Make sure there's no survivors." Survivor Jackson Kabura

said the men entered wearing military fatigues. The bar shooting left 39 people dead. The accused later claimed the massacre's "sponsors" were top security official General Maurice Mbonimpa, deputy police chief General Gervais Ndirakobuca and the commander of a special police unit, Colonel Desire Uwamahoro.
-2011   Nov 21, Burundi security forces shot dead 18 "armed bandits" in clashes in the eastern province of Cankuzo, part of a new rebellion based in Ruvubu National   Park.
-2011   Nov 22, A Burundi rights group, the Government Action Observatory (OAG), said government-backed death squads have killed more than 300 members of a former rebel group and opposition supporters in covert operations   over   the   past   five   months.
-2011   Nov 27, Gunmen in Burundi murdered Sister Luckrecija Mamic, a Croatian nun, and an Italian charity worker in an apparent botched robbery and kidnapping. Sister Carla Brianza was later shot dead while Sister Carla Brianza, an Italian nun, fought off her attackers and escaped with relatively minor wounds. Two men, aged 20 and 24, were arrested for the attack after a shootout.
-2012   May 2, Burundi blocked Human Rights Watch from holding a press conference to release a report on the country's political violence, which it blamed on state agents   and   armed   opposition   groups.
-2012   May 5, In Burundi an armed gang kidnapped, killed and dismembered overnight an albino girl (15) in Burundi's 18th such slaying in less than four years. "Albinos Sans Frontieres" said the government was failing to protect albinos and said everyone sentenced to prison in

the   killings   had   escaped.
-2012   Jun 20, A Burundian court sentenced journalist Hassan Ruvakuki and 13 others to life in prison on terrorism charges for a November attack launched from across the Tanzanian border, a ruling criticized by media watchdogs.
-2013   Sep 12, A UN official said at least 25,000 Burundian refugees living in Tanzania have been forcibly repatriated over the past month, describing a "dramatic" humanitarian   situation.
-2013   Sep 13, Burundi opened an investigation into claims that a former ethnic Hutu rebel leader ordered the massacre of Congolese refugees in an attack almost a decade ago. The Banyamulenge, an ethnic Tutsi tribe from neighboring Democratic Republic of Congo, in August accused Agathon Rwasa of ordering the killing of 166 Banyamulenge seeking refuge inside a camp in Burundi   in   2004.
-2013   Nov 10, Burundi officials said police have discovered dozens of human skulls during a search of the home of an Italian expatriate. Giuseppe Favaro, has been in custody since late October after he was caught trying to   export   two   skulls   to   Thailand.
-2014   Feb 11, The Burundi Red Cross said torrential rains and landslides have left at least 77 people dead and about   12,000   displaced.
-2014   Mar 12, Burundi charged opposition leader Alexis Sinduhije, who is on the run from police, and 71 party supporters with rebellion following March 8 clashes.
-2014   Jul, On the Burundi-Rwanda border corpses started coming with rotting bodies and bound limbs or stuffed in sacks, floating on the glittering waters of Lake

Rweru. Fishermen report seeing as many as 40 bodies. In 2006 the bodies of Burundian opponents murdered in political violence were thrown into various rivers in the country.

-2014   Sep 8, The Italian foreign ministry said 3 missionary nuns have been found slain in their convent in Burundi.

-2014   Dec 20, Burundi's National Intelligence Service detained Brice Nzohabonayo in the capital Bujumbura shortly after his brother Bertrand Nzohabonayo attacked a   police   station   in   Joue-les-Tours,   France

-2015   Jan 4, A Burundi military official said at least 105 rebels have been killed after a cross-border attack from the Democratic Republic of Congo following five days of non-stop military operations. Five gunmen dressed in military fatigues burst into a bar and shot dead 3 ruling party activists before torching the local party office in the eastern   Gisuru   region.

-2015   Feb 3, In Burundi some 150 journalists and civil rights activists demonstrated to demand the release of a radio station boss accused of complicity in the murder of three   Italian   nuns   last   September.

-2015   Feb 12, Human Rights Watch said Burundian troops executed at least 47 surrendered rebels last month, part of a "broader pattern" of violence coming ahead of key   elections.

-2015   Feb 19, In Burundi thousands marched through the capital in one of the largest demonstrations in recent years after the release of Bob Rugurika, a popular journalist and government critic from jail, months ahead of   key   elections.

-2015   Apr 17, Burundi police fired tear gas and water cannon to disperse protesters calling for the president not to run for a third term.
-2015   Apr 26, Burundian police shot dead 2 protesters and wounded at least one other, in demonstrations against the president seeking a third term.
-2015   Apr 27, Burundi authorities arrested a leading dissident and shut down the main independent radio station as they battled a second day of demonstrations against a bid by the president to cling to power for a third term. The Red Cross said at least 6 people have been killed in the street clashes.
-2015   Apr 28, In Burundi police fired tear gas and shot in the air to disperse hundreds of people protesting in the outskirts of Bujumbura against President Pierre Nkurunziza's decision to run for a third term. The UN said more than 5,000 Burundians fled to Rwanda over the weekend.
-2015   Apr 30, In Burundi at least nine protestors were hurt in Bujumbura in renewed clashes over a bid by the country's president to stand for a third term. A soldier died and a civilian was hurt when an intelligence officer opened fire near a barricade erected by protesters in Bujumbura.
-2015   May 1, In Burundi 2 police officers and a civilian were killed in two grenade attacks late today in Bujumbura.
-2015   May 4, Burundi police shot dead at least 3 demonstrators and wounded dozens of others, in running battles with protesters angry at a bid by President Pierre Nkurunziza to extend his rule.
-2015   May 6, The UN said nearly 40,000 refugees have

fled Burundi to neighboring Rwanda, Tanzania and the Democratic Republic of the Congo in the last month, amid protests against President Pierre Nkurunziza's bid for a   third   term.
-2015   May 7, In Burundi at least 4 people were killed in clashes over the president's bid for a third term. Protesters burned a man alive in Bujumbura, saying he was a member of the ruling party's youth wing which had attacked   them   during   their   demonstrations.
-2015   May 11, In Burundi about 2,000 people marched through a neighborhood of Bujumbura as police looked on, breaking the government's ban on any further street protests against President Pierre Nkurunziza's bid for a third term   in   power.
-2015   May 13, Burundi Major General Godefroid Niyombare said he had deposed President Pierre Nkurunziza for seeking an unconstitutional third term in office, and was working with civil society groups to form a transitional government. Niyombare was fired as Nkurunziza's intelligence chief in February. President Pierre Nkurunziza was abroad at an African summit in Tanzania. The Major General Godefroid Niyombare one of the orphans of 1972 unrecognized genocide strongly believes that the problem of Burundi is the lack of visionary and well   accepted   leadership.
-2015   May 14, Burundi's armed forces chief announced that an attempted coup against President Pierre Nkurunziza had failed, although the claim was quickly denied by opponents of the central African nation's leader. Rival factions of Burundi's army fought intense battles for control of the capital. 12 soldiers who

backed the coup were killed. President, Nkurunziza returned to Burundi and a deputy coup leader said the attempted coup has failed.
-2015   May 15, The UN refugee agency said more than 105,000 people have fled Burundi to Tanzania, Rwanda and the Democratic Republic of Congo, following an attempted coup and protests.
-2015   May 16, Burundi officials said five generals have been arrested for plotting a failed coup led by Maj. Gen. Godefroid Niyombare, who remained in hiding in Kigali, Rwanda.
-2015   May 19, Burundi police fired tear gas and beat protesters who were demanding President Pierre Nkurunziza end his bid for a third term. Rights groups say at least 20 people have died in three weeks of clashes between security forces and protesters.
-2015   May 20, A Burundi army officer said police killed a soldier who was trying act as a buffer between police and protesters, who are demonstrating against the president's bid for a third term in office.
-2015   May 21, In Burundi street battles and gunfire erupted again in Bujumbura as protesters against President Pierre Nkurunziza rejected calls for calm. 2 protesters were killed bringing to 20 the number of deaths witnessed by the Red Cross over the last month.
-2015   May 23, In Burundi opposition politician Zedi Feruzi and a body guard were killed in a drive-by shooting. Thousands of people attended his funeral the next day.
-2015   May 31, In Tanzania African leaders began talks in their second summit in a month aimed at restoring

peace   in   Burundi.
-2015   Jun 19, Rights activists said at least 77 people
have been killed in Burundi in clashes with security forces
since the start of antigovernment protests in April.
-2015   Jun 22, In Burundi 4 people died and at least 30
were wounded in an overnight grenade attack on a bar
in the country's northern region of Ngozi. Three people
were   arrested   following   the   attack.
-2015   Jun 25, Burundian students broke into the US
embassy to escape police as one of the country's vice
presidents announced he had fled to Belgium.
-2015   Jun 27, In Burundi witnesses in Jabe
neighborhood in of Bujumbura, reported intense gunfire
late that day in an apparent police crackdown on areas
seen as hosting anti-government protesters. Two people
were killed in attacks believed to have been carried out
by   police.
-2015   Jul 10, Burundi's government said it backed
regional calls to postpone controversial polls, but only by
a few days, saying it had asked the election commission
to implement the delay. Burundian soldiers clashed with
gunmen in a northern region near Rwanda. Government
soldiers killed 31 suspected rebels and captured another
170   in   Kayanza   province.
-2015   Jul 12, In Burundi a regional governor said the
army has captured scores of gunmen and killed others in
two   days   of   clashes   in   the   north.
-2015   Jul 21, Polls for Burundi's presidential election
opened to the news that 3 people had been killed
overnight. On July 24 the election commission announced
that President Pierre Nkurunziza won his controversial third

consecutive   term   in   office
-2015   Jul 22, A supporter of Burundi's opposition was
shot dead, a victim of electoral violence as the country
awaits results of the presidential election amid unrest due
to President Pierre Nkurunziza's bid for a third term.
-2015   Aug 2, In Burundi General Adolphe
Nshimirimana, a close aide to President Pierre Nkurunziza,
was killed in a rocket attack on his car in Bujumbura.
-2015   Aug 3, Burundian human rights activist Pierre-
Claver Mbonimpa was shot in the face as he made his
way home from work by a gunman on a motorbike. He
publicly opposed Pres. Pierre Nkurunziza's controversial
and successful bid for a third term last month. Mbonimpa
survived and his condition the next day was reported
stable.
-2015   Aug 5, In Burundi Come Harerimana, a local
leader of the ruling party, was attacked and killed in
Bujumbura, the third high-profile attack in three days.
-2015   Aug 13, Burundi's ruling party termed the
controversial re-election of President Pierre Nkurunziza (51)
a "divine miracle", as the opposition accused him of
declaring war by clinging to power. Meanwhile violence
continued unabated with at least 3 people killed in the
last   24   hours.
-2015   Aug 15, In Burundi unidentified gunmen shot
and killed Col. Jean Bikomagu, the former army chief of
staff, in the second high-profile killing this month amid
chaos linked to the disputed reelection of President Pierre
Nkurunziza.
-2015   Aug 18, In Burundi 4 people were killed in
Bujumbura   as   violence   persisted   following   the

controversial re-election of President Pierre Nkurunziza.
-2015	Aug 20, Burundi President Pierre Nkurunziza was sworn in for a third term without any fanfare or even a public	announcement	beforehand.
-2015	Sep 2, In Burundi anti-government protesters resumed in some neighborhoods in the capital after residents accused the police of harassment. At least 4 people	were	killed	in	the	renewed	clashes.
-2015	Sep 7, In Burundi the spokesman for an opposition party was shot and killed outside his home in Bujumbura.
-2015	Sep 11, In Burundi the head of the armed forces survived an assassination attempt in the capital Bujumbura. At least seven people were killed in the attack.
-2015	Sep 16, A Burundi official said more than 100 men in a central province have been arrested in two days by security forces trying to prevent Burundians from being recruited	to	fight	the	government.
-2015	Sep 24, In Burundi unidentified gunmen raided a police station in Bujumbura. One of the attackers was killed	with	no	other	casualties.
-2015	Oct 3, In Burundi at least a dozen civilians were killed in clashes between police and anti-government protesters	in	Bujumbura.
-2015	Oct 9, In Burundi unknown gunmen killed Pascal Nshirimana, the son-in-law of prominent human rights activist Pierre Claver Mbonimpa, who openly opposed President Pierre Nkurunziza's controversial bid for a third term	in	office.
-2015	Oct 13, In Burundi 9 civilians, including a staff

member of the International Organization for Migration (IOM), were shot to death reportedly at close range. 2 police officers also died during exchanges of heavy gunfire in Bujumbura.
-2015   Oct 26, In Burundi gunmen hurled grenades and battled with police in a series of deadly clashes, the latest violence since the controversial re-election of President Pierre Nkurunziza. Police killed a "madman" who tried to attack officers with a machete in Bujumbura. Over the next 24 hours more than a dozen people were killed in clashes between security forces and citizens.
-2015   Nov 2, Burundi President Pierre Nkurunziza gave civilians five days to surrender any illegal weapons or face tough action by the police. 2 more bodies were discovered in Bujumbura. 9 people have been killed in gunfights with security forces since Oct 31.
-2015   Nov 5, In Burundi some residents fled their neighborhood in Bujumbura after they found four bodies on the streets, part of a wave of killings associated with President Pierre Nkurunziza's re-election for a third term.
-2015   Nov 8, In Burundi gunmen at least 9 people were killed in an attack at a bar in Bujumbura hours before police launched house-to-house searches for weapons. Families were fleeing their homes in the capital, over fears the government will unleash a fresh wave of bloodletting as part of a crackdown to stamp out resistance to the president.
-2015   Nov 16, In Burundi three grenades exploded in different parts of the capital following a night of violence in which 5 people, including a policeman, were killed. 60 injured people were treated after suffering injuries in

grenade   explosions.
-2015   Nov 22, Burundi police said at least 5 people
were killed in overnight clashes. Residents reported a
battle at the president's office in the capital Bujumbura
which has been plagued by violence since a disputed
presidential   election.
-2015   Nov 23, The US said it would impose sanctions on
four current and former Burundi government officials,
including the minister of public security and the leader of
a failed coup, because of violence in Burundi.
-2015   Nov 27, In Burundi attackers shot at a lawmaker
from the ruling party as he drove to parliament, killing one
police   officer   and   wounding   others.
-2015   Nov 28, In Burundi Colonel Serges Kabanyura
was wounded in an attack by unidentified gunmen on his
way   to   Bujumbura.
-2015   Nov 29, In Burundi gunmen in Bujumbura shot
dead army Major Salvator Katihabwa and wounded the
husband   of   the   senate's   deputy   speaker.
-2015   Dec 2, In Burundi at least 7 people were killed
over the last 24 hours in gun battles and grenade blasts
with   bodies   found   dumped   on   the   streets.
-2015   Dec 4, Burundi police shot dead 3 attackers and
arrested three others when they foiled an attempt to
ambush and assassinate a top police officer in the
capital.
-2015   Dec 9, In Burundi at least 7 people were killed in
Bujumbura during a night of violence in flashpoint districts
where months of protests took place against President
Pierre   Nkurunziza.
-2015   Dec 11, In Burundi gunmen stormed three

military installations before dawn. At least 15 people were killed as gunfire and explosions rocked the capital. 87 people were reported killed in the violence.
-2015   Dec 12, Burundi residents awoke to find at least 39 dead bodies scattered in the streets of Bujumbura, a day after coordinated armed assaults on three military installations. 87 people were killed in an escalation of the violence surrounding the disputed third term of President Pierre   Nkurunziza.
-2015   Dec 18, The African Union said it will send a 5,000 strong force to stop violence in troubled Burundi, giving Bujumbura a four-day deadline to agree but warning   it   would   send   troops   anyway.
-2015   Dec 20, Burundi's government said it would not agree to the deployment of African Union peacekeepers, warning that they would be seen as an invasion force.
-2015   Dec 22, Burundi's government rejected a proposed African Union peacekeeping mission already dubbed   an   "invasion   force"   by   parliament.
-2015   Dec 23, Burundi's rebels came together for the first time as a force aimed at ousting President Pierre Nkurunziza, after months of bloodshed in the troubled central African country. The rebels have called themselves the Republican Forces of Burundi, or "Forebu" from its name in French, Les Forces Republicaines du Burundi.
-2015   Dec 26, In Burundi thousands of supporters of the president protested against the African Union's plan to deploy 5,000 peacekeepers to quell the country's escalating   unrest.
-2016   Jan 1, In Burundi at least one person was killed

and a dozen injured in a series of grenade attacks in Bujumbura.

-2016   Jan 13, In Burundi Army Capt. Idi Omar Bahenda and police Brig. Jean Claude Niyongabo were killed in a gunfight with military forces in the Kiyenzi area of Bujumbura. Bahenda was wanted for recruiting rebels opposed to the government.

-2016   Jan 15, The UN said it has documented cases of Burundi's security forces gang-raping women during searches of opposition supporters' houses and heard witness testimony of mass graves.

-2016   Jan 18, In Burundi 3 people were killed late that day in a grenade attack on a bar in Bujumbura.

-2016   Jan 30, African leaders met in Addis Ababa in a bid to end armed crises, including in troubled Burundi, with an unprecedented vote on deploying a 5,000-strong peacekeeping force despite Burundi's vehement opposition.

-2016   Feb 3, A confidential report to the UN Security Council accused Rwanda of recruiting and training Burundian refugees with the goal of ousting Burundian President Pierre Nkurunziza.

-2016   Feb 12, Rwanda said it will send Burundian refugees to other countries, after the United States said that they were being recruited from camps to fight on behalf of the Burundian opposition.

-2016   Feb 13, In central Burundi two people loyal to the ruling party were "executed" overnight in Gacimbirigongo.

-2016   Feb 13, In Burundi a grenade attack late today on a military base in Bujumbura killed a child and

wounded his father and one other person.
-2016   Feb 15, Insurgents in Burundi hurled a series of grenades, killing a child and wounding at least 30 people in the latest in a string of attacks.
-2016   Feb 21, In Burundi 2 people were killed late that day in a gun attack in a bar.
-2016   Feb 22, In Burundi one person had died and another was wounded in a grenade attack at a Bujumbura market just hours before the arrival of UN Secretary-General Ban Ki-moon who was trying to end the bloodshed over President Pierre Nkurunziza's disputed re-election.
-2016   Feb 25, A delegation of five African heads of state arrived in Bujumbura at the start of a two-day visit to push for talks to end Burundi's deep political crisis.
-2016   Feb 27, The African Union said it will deploy rights observers and military monitors to violence-plagued Burundi following a visit to the country by five African leaders.
-2016   Mar 2, Former Tanzanian president Benjamin Mkapa was named as the new mediator for talks to end a nearly year-long crisis in neighboring Burundi by the regional East African Community (EAC).
-2016   Mar 14, The European Union said it is suspending direct financial support for the Burundian government after concluding that it had not done enough to find a political solution to conflict that has so far cost more than 400 lives.
-2016   Mar 22, In Burundi Maj. Didier Muhimpundu was killed after being shot several times in a bar in Bujumbura. Lieutenant Colonel Darius Ikurakure was shot dead by an

assassin dressed in a military uniform inside the ministry compound in Bujumbura. The rebel group FOREBU, led by a former officer who launched an abortive coup, later claimed responsibility for the death of Ikurakure.
-2016   Mar 30, In Burundi Jacques Bihozagara, a former Rwandan ambassador to France and Belgium and an ex-government minister, died in a jail where he was being held on suspicion of spying, adding to cross-border tensions that have increased dangerously in recent months. He had been held on espionage charges since December.
-2016   Apr 11, In Burundi gunmen killed at least 5 people and wounded seven when they opened fire on a market late that day in the eastern Ruyigi region.
-2016   Apr 13, In Burundi Phocas Bakaza, a member of the ruling CNDD-FDD party, was shot dead in Mutimbuzi area near the capital Bujumbura. Two people were soon arrested   in   connection   with   the   attack.
-2016   Apr 14, A Burundi soldier was killed when an armed group attacked a military camp northwest of Bujumbura.
-2016   Apr 16, In Burundi 4 members of the country's ruling party were killed in an attack in continuing violence associated with the extended tenure of Pres. Pierre Nkurunziza.
-2016   Apr 20, In Burundi gunmen ambushed Colonel Emmanuel Buzubona as he traveled on the back of a motorbike to his home in Bujumbura. Soldiers on patrol killed two people in a clash with an armed group in Kivumu village in Mugamba southern district, 60 km southeast   of   Bujumbura.

-2016   Apr 25, In Burundi Athanase Kararuza, a Tutsi general and security advisor to the vice president, was killed in an attack by heavily-armed men, along with his wife   and   daughter   in   Bujumbura.
-2016   Apr 25, In eastern Burundi nearly 30 schoolchildren and their supervisors were killed and many more injured when their truck crashed outside Musongati.
-2016   May 16, Rwanda officials said over 1,500 Burundians have been expelled in recent days, amid worsening   relations   between   the   neighbors.
-2016   May 24, In Burundi gunmen killed 3 people including a retired army colonel and a police chief, in continuing violence associated with Pres. Pierre Nkurunziza's   extended   time   in   power.
-2016   Jun 2, The United States said it has sanctioned Burundi military commander Marius Ngendabanka, security official Ignace Sibomana and rebel leader Edouard Nshimirimana for engaging in actions or policies that threaten the peace, security or stability of the East African   country.
-2016   Jul 13, In Burundi Hafsa Mossi, a former minister in President Pierre Nkurunziza's government, was "shot by criminals" in Bujumbura. She was a member of the East African   Legislative   Assembly.
-2016   Jul 29, The UN Security Council agreed to send a contingent of 228 United Nations police to Burundi to control the continuing violence and to protect human rights   in   the   East   African   nation.
-2016   Jul 30, In Burundi more than 1,000 people participated in a government-backed demonstration in the capital, Bujumbura, to protest France's proposal

passed by UN Security Council to deploy UN police to the country.

-2016   Aug 2, Burundi said it would refuse to allow United Nations police onto its territory to monitor the security and human rights situation after the UN Security Council voted to send 228 officers.

-2016   Nov 24, Burundi's government refused to cooperate with a UN inquiry into months of political violence, saying accusations of abuses by its officials were part of a political plot. The UN released a report by independent experts in September identifying government officials suspected of ordering political opposition to be tortured or killed.

-2016   Nov 26, In Burundi thousands of people took part in street protests across the country in support of the government's opposition to United Nations investigators who are looking into alleged human rights abuses in the east African country.

-2016   Dec 22, Democratic Republic of Congo troops killed 10 soldiers from neighboring Burundi after they crossed the border overnight in pursuit of rebels.

-2016   Dec 23, Burundi's parliament passed a law imposing strict controls on international non-governmental organizations after President Pierre Nkurunziza accused such groups of backing an insurrection against him.

-2017   Jan 1, In Burundi a gunman killed Emmanuel Niyonkuru (54), the country's environment and water minister early today, the first senior government figure to be murdered in nearly two years of political violence.

-2017   Mar 13, Burundi's health minister said about 700 people have died from malaria in Burundi so far this year.

He said authorities have registered 1.8 million infections in a rising epidemic.

-2017   Mar 29, The UN said a malaria outbreak has killed more than 4,000 people in Burundi this year, a significant increase over the 700 cited by the country's health ministry on March 13.

-2017   Apr 18, The UN rights chief condemned the feared youth wing of Burundi's ruling party for repeatedly calling for the rape and murder of opposition supporters. Human Rights Watch has accused the Imbonerakure of being involved in assaults on opposition members, gang-rapes of women and torture. The UN regularly refers to them as a militia.

-2017   May 17, In Burundi an unidentified man threw a grenade into a house in Bujumbura, killing three people believed to be members of the ruling party's youth wing.

-2017   Jun 15, Burundi denied UN allegations that said its security forces and government-allied militia are continuing to torture and kill opponents.

-2017   Jul 9, In Burundi a grenade attack late that day killed eight people and wounded 50 others in a village in northern Kayanza province.

-2017   Jul 18, In Washington, DC, six teens from Burundi went missing while competing in an int'l. robotics competition. Two of them were seen crossing into Canada and foul play was not suspected.

-2017   Aug 17, In Burundi grenade attacks on two bars killed at least three people and wounded 27 others in Bujumbura.

-2017   Sep 4, UN investigators accused Burundi's government of crimes against humanity, including

executions and torture, and urged the International Criminal Court to open a case "as soon as possible". Burundi formally announced it was withdrawing from the court, with the move set to take effect on October 27.
-2017   Sep 15, in eastern Congo DRC at least 36 Burundian refugees were killed in clashes with Congolese security forces in the town of Kamanyola over plans to send some of them home. One Congolese officer was killed.
-2017   Sep 29, The UN Human Rights Council voted to extend the mission of an international probe into atrocities in Burundi, overriding strong pushback from the government accused of crimes against humanity.
-2017   Oct 24, Burundi's cabinet backed a constitutional change that would allow its president to stay in office until 2034, widening a political rift that has driven the country progressively deeper into crisis.
-2017   Oct 27, Burundi became the first country to withdraw from the International Criminal Court. Officials said the court's prosecutor will move ahead with an examination of the East African nation's deadly political turmoil.
-2017   Nov 9, The International Criminal Court (ICC) approved a prosecution request to investigate war crimes allegedly committed in Burundi by the government and government-linked groups against political foes from April 2015 to October 2017.

-2018 Sep 17, United Nations investigators (the UN independent investigation on Burundi, UNIIB) accused the government of Burundi of gross human rights violations, following a nine-month inquiry into the alleged torture and murder of government opponents in the troubled African state.

CHAP II.THE ORIGIN AND ROOT OF DEEP WOUNDS, TRAUMA AND EVIL OF BURUNDI NATION

"This quests to the United Nations Human Rights Commission to Mandate a Diligent investigations into the Burundi 1972 Mass Killings of Hutus in Order to Recognize them As a Genocide against Hutus under International Law."

1.The context

On April 28, 1972, Colonel Michel Micombero, President of Burundi, dissolved his government, declared martial law and unleashed the next day an all-out military repression on the Hutu population in a carnage which would eventually leave more than 300000 people killed and hundreds of thousands more forced to cross the borders and seek security in neighbouring countries1. Everything that this poor, small central African nation of about 4 million inhabitants could count as educated or otherwise skilled Hutu was targeted for systematic elimination. From schoolteachers to local clerks, university students and government officials, every Hutu with any form of education was perceived as posing a threat to the Tutsi

---

Kiraranganya (1985, p 76) cited in Lemarchand, R. (2002).Le génocide de 1972 au Burundi. *Les silences de l'Histoire:Cahier d'Etudes Africaines,* 167, pp 551-568.

political hegemony and was therefore apprehended, abducted and tortured before being atrociously killed. Hutu members of the armed forces, from commissioned officers down to private soldiers, were seen as a particular threat because of their potential to lead an armed insurrection and were therefore systematically executed without any form of due process. The slaughter went on for several months. By the end of August, more than 200,000 people had reportedly been killed, although the precise total number of victims remains disputed (Lemarchand, 2008). [2],

The brutal repression was carried out by both the military and the UPRONA party youth wing, the Jeunesses Révolutuonnaires Rwagasore (JRR). Under the instigation of the president's extremist entourage consisting of the ministers Arthémon Simbananiye (Foreign Affairs) Albert Shibura (Interior and Justice), François Gisamare (Education), André Yanda (Secretary General of the party Uprona) and Sylvère Nzohabonayo, officers (camp commander Bujumbura) Ndabemeye Thomas (Chief of Staff of the army), Jean-Baptiste Bagaza (Deputy Chief of Staff of the army), Alexis Nimubona officers Nduwingoma Samuel, Joseph Rwuri, Gervais Gahuragiza, Damascus Ngendakuriyo, Micombero had organised massacres targeted at eliminating all Hutu intellectuals. The trigger

[2]Lemarchand, R.(2008).The Burundi Killings of 1972: Online Encyclopedia of Mass Violence. http://migs.concordia.ca/documents/The-Burundi-Killings-of-1972Lemarchand.The%20Burundi%20Killings%20of%201972%20by%20Ren%C3%A9%20Lemarchandpdf. Last accessed June 24, 2016.

for the onslaught was a Hutu-led rebellion that had broken out in the south of the country.

Since April 27, the country was indeed undergoing an insurrection led by Hutu rebels around the southern regions of Nyanza-Lac in Makamba province, as well as Rumonge, and other parts of Bururi province. The Hutu insurgents estimated to be around only one thousand, according to the account of a French helicopter pilot who flew missions of the Burundian government against them, had tried to establish and proclaim an own republic where their civil rights would be protected and massacred some 1200 Tutsi in the process[3]. For long, their frustrations of being denied the same civil rights as their Tutsi fellow citizens had been building up as they saw their kin and representatives purged from the army and the government ranks. Indeed, tensions between these two ethnic groups had been ingrained ever since the colonial time, when the German and the Belgian governments favoured the Tutsi and restricted the rights of Hutus. As recalled by Des Forges (2011, p.27 & p. 87) favouring the Tutsi ruling class at the expense of the basic rights of the Hutu majority had been a deliberate policy of the German imperial government[4] and that of Catholic

---

3The Republic of Matyazo was proclaimed by insurgents but lasted only a few days before it was destroyed by the crushing repression of the Burundian army.

[4] Richard Kandt, the German resident in Kigali, stated the official position of the German government towards the Hutu-Tutsi injustices in 1911: "The policy of the Imperial Government and therefore of its Residency is based upon up- holding and strengthening the authority of the Princes and the Sultan under all circumstances, even when in the process the Wahutu must suffer injustice." Except when pressed particularly hard by the missionaries to hear a case, the Germans generally insisted that all affairs be judged first by notables and be brought to them only on appeal

missionaries, a policy only briefly reversed by the Belgian colonial regime after the defeat of the Germans in WWI but quickly reinstated ever since. After only a few months of attempts to redress the injustices against the Hutus, the Belgians had reverted to same imperial policy, which became integrally endorsed by colonial administration in 1917.

The Catholic Church was largely complicit in nurturing Burundi's ethnic divisions. Catholic schools, for instance, were largely reserved for the children of the Tutsis elite[5]. As was the case in Rwanda, the White missionaries also became a power by themselves within the colonial structure by acquiring large plots of land and acting like the ruling Tutsi notables in exploiting the Hutu population. Under Belgian colonial rule, the minority Tutsi elite, which identified itself with an ethnical group accounting for roughly 14 percent of the population, was favoured and given enormous privileges enabling its members to gain control of the military, government and most importantly, land. Hutu chiefs who controlled land at that time were progressively stripped of their rights and claims, which were granted to Tutsi without any form of compensation. Years of systematic injustices supported by the Tutsi who benefited from these unearned privileges further pitted oppressed Hutu against the Tutsis collaborating with

---

(Des Forges, A. 2011. Defeat is the only bad news. Rwanda under Musinga 1896-1931.University of Wisconsin Press. p. 87).
5(Keenan, 2005).The blood cries out. Foreign Policy.http://foreignpolicy.com/2015/03/27/the-blood-cries-out-burundi-land-conflict/. Last accessed on June 24, 2016.

colonizers to exploit the population masses. As the Tutsis continued to build on their government and military monopoly, the tensions had exacerbated since the assassination in 1961 of the first democratically elected Prime Minister Louis Rwagasore, whose party, UPRONA, had won the parliamentary elections with equal numbers of Hutu and Tutsi representatives.

After a continuous process that saw the Hutu being progressively eliminated from the power structure of the post-independence government, a small group of frustrated Hutu intellectuals, presumably operating from Tanzania, launched a rebellion aimed at retrieving power from the ruling Tutsi minority. In a matter of a few days insurgents carried out attacks that killed hundreds of Tutsis. Immediately after the insurgency had broken out on April 27, the Micombero regime seized the moment to scale up the already existing process of purging the state institutions of all Hutus, with the deliberate intention to eliminate any Hutu intellectual having the capacity to challenge the Tutsi monopoly of power and claim civil rights for his fellow citizens. Weapons had already been distributed, especially by Shibura, to the Tutsis living in the Tanganyika coastal towns of Rumonge and Nyanza–Lac, as if the rebellion had been anticipated. Those weapons would later prove to be the ones used to massacre Hutu civilians. The rapidity with which the regime reacted to exterminate the Hutu population after crushing the rebellion has raised serious suspicions that the massacres were planned beforehand and the rebellion was only instigated to serve as a pretext to start the killings. Reports by the government media also suggested that Hutu officers had attempted to overthrow the regime, which served as another pretext to execute all Hutu commissioned and non-commissioned officers serving in the army. Subsequently, all Hutus in rank and file were also executed so as to replace them by Tutsi and leave an ethnically cleansed army.

The scale of massacres and he extreme brutality with which the extermination of all Hutu elite was carried out has led many observers to characterize this cruel repression as a genocide (Lemarchand, 2002). Some have used the term *selective genocide* to emphasise the systematic targeting of mostly educated Hutus in order to ensure that no Hutu would ever be able to marshal the required resources to stand up against Tutsi-led government injustices and claim the rights of the masses. Among the few who immediately qualified the indiscriminate and brutal repression as genocide, was the then Belgian Prime Minister Gaston Eyskens. However, other observers have continued to show reticence and reservations about using such a qualification, either because of their own strategic interests, or as a result of their historic and contextual bias in the civil rights tensions between the Tutsi-dominated regimes and the population masses. The United Nations called it simply a tragedy. Lemarchand (2002) attributes the silence of the international community to the Cold War context of that moment, which made the Western former colonial powers inclined to favour dictators in that region of the globe and turn a blind eye on such atrocities as long as the dictator served their direct strategic interests.

The low media coverage at the time of the crimes and afterwards as well as the commensurate lack of interest for the region on the part of the Western public at large, has given the successive Burundi regimes dominated by the perpetrators time and opportunity to cover up their horrendous crimes and so prevent the indignation of the international community from spreading in the open. Successive Tutsi-led governments of Burundi have succeeded in meticulously suppressing evidence and therefore hiding their crimes. As a result, the international community has failed to grasp the genocidal character of these massacres and has so far been hesitant to thoroughly investigate and recognised them as such. One of the consequences of this reluctance has been that the victims and the survivors have never been officially recognised and have therefore continued to suffer the sequels of this traumatic experience, without a legal framework enabling the country to extend psychological and material support to them. Such support is however indispensable to alleviate the immense suffering of survivors, albeit only slightly, and start the healing process.

With the end of the Tutsi monopoly on power enshrined in the 2005 Constitution, it is very crucial for the new democratic society of Burundi to confront the demons of its past and recognise the genocide that destroyed the lives of an entire generation of educated Hutus and left their families in such a disarray that they are still undergoing the consequences of their traumatic deprivation of dignity. While the work of the Truth and Reconciliation Committee (CVR) has begun with the aim to bring to light all historic events that have contributed to sickening the Burundian society, the crimes committed during the 1972 genocide have been of such a deleterious character that they ought to be examined separately, if Burundi is ever to be healed of its historic wounds and its deep seated ethnic mistrusts. The request to recognise the 1972 genocide against the Hutus committed by the Micombero regime must thus be understood in the context of a comprehensive effort aimed to heal the Burundian society of the painful consequences of its troubled and violent history. For Burundi to move forward in ethnic harmony with hope for a brighter future, it cannot afford the luxury of failing to understand this traumatic episode of its history and appropriately deal with its consequences.

2 Historical background

The 1972 genocide took place in a context of recurrent ethnic tensions that had been building up since the colonial period. The ethnic composition of Burundi through the 1960s and 1970s were roughly 86 percent Hutu, 13 percent Tutsi, and 1 percent Twa (Mann, 2005)[6]. For most of this period, the Tutsi maintained a near monopoly on senior government and military positions. While pre-colonial Burundi was essentially ruled by a Tutsi king and a Tutsi royal aristocracy (Ganwa), the ethnic tensions were relatively limited as Hutu were allowed to participate in many public functions, including the process of selecting the new king (mwami) and the intendancy of his royal estates. The Bahutu were in charge of most religious duties in the kingdom and in that capacity, retained a significant influence (Ghislain, 1970)[7]. The royal family also claimed to have mixed Hutu-Tutsi origins, although the royal princes invariably chose the future queen mothers from among unmixed Tutsi clans. This ensured a significant influence for the Tutsi, especially those belonging to the clans from which the royal spouses were selected. In contrast, the Tutsi Bahima of the Bururi region in the south of the country, from which the 3 successive post-independence military rulers of Burundi would emerge, had been systematically excluded from power positions for centuries. This partly explains why the political tensions that were later to emerge after independence, would follow not only the fault lines of ethnic Hutu-Tutsi cleavage, but also, within the Tutsi ethnic group, between the Tutsi- Hima from the south and the

---

[6] Man, M. 2005: The Dark Side of Democracy, p. 431.

[7] Ghislain, J. 1970. La féodalité au Burundi. Académie Royale des Sciences d'Outre-Mer, Bruxelles.

Tutsi-Banyaruguru from the north of the country, as the latter were considered supporters of the monarchy. The rise of Tutsi Bahima in the structure of the Burundian army provided them thus with the opportunity to grab the power they thought they had been denied for long and would sow the seeds of the 1972 genocide against Hutu, coupled with the regicide (the last king of Burundi, Ntare V, who had been deposed since captain Micombero's coup in November 1966, was killed on April 30, 1972, at the beginning of the genocide against Hutus, with the view to crush any hope of their potential rallying around the former monarch).

Until the arrival of the Germans, who came to incorporate the country into the imperial Deutsch Ostafrika protectorate, Burundi was a feudal kingdom, in which power was highly decentralised. German officers who had been sent to administer the territory described the political situation they found in Burundi as an anarchic kingdom with recurrent intestine wars, unlike their northern neighbour, Rwanda, where the royal power was highly centralised in the hands of a Tutsi monarchy. The kingdom of Burundi, as it was at the arrival of the first Europeans, had reached its final dimensions under the mwami Ntare-Ruyenzi, who had enjoyed a long and glorious reign in the first half of the 19th century. He had doubled the size of the domain he inherited from his father. The Burundian kings, the Bami, ascended to the throne with successive dynastic names of respectively Ntare, Mwezi, Mutaga and

Mwambutsa. Royal descendants of those kings bore respectively the clan names Abaganwa *batare, bezi, bataga* and *bambutsa*. The king held a relatively week royal power, which was balanced by the local authority of Baganwa, a class of aristocrats descended from previous generations of royal princes, who controlled vast domains. At the advent of each new king, who traditionally was designated among the younger teenage sons of the old king, the previous generation of Baganwa, whose clan name corresponded to the dynastic name of the new monarch lost its princely privileges to a new one, and became Abafasoni, i.e. notables of high rank. The ruling class was therefore renewed each time a new monarch came to power, but this renewal and removal of the previous generation of Baganwa to make place for new ones often went with intrigues and violence. In this process, however, some powerful Baganwa who were close relatives of the royal family or were otherwise influential, managed to retain control of their domains.

The pre-colonial power sharing arrangements reflected the initial role division between the Hutu majority and the Tutsi minority, which had come into existence as a result alliance often concluded with interethnic marriages. The weak and decentralised structure of the power ensured that tensions between the central power and the population masses remained relatively limited. Rather than interethnic, power related violence and intrigues erupted thus mainly within the ruling aristocracy, with various claimants jostling to keep or acquire aristocratic domains and privileges. Unlike Rwanda, ethnic tensions between Hutus and Tutsis in Burundi had thus only built up under, and had been exacerbated by the Belgian colonisation, which had sought to enforce a systematic preference for Tutsi in the colonial administration and a progressive side-lining of Hutus from any position of power or influence. Also playing a highly negative role in these tensions was the arrival of Rwandan Tutsi refugee who had lost their monopoly hold on power after Rwandan Hutus led a successful social revolution to abolish the political hegemony of an oppressive Tutsi ruling class. Rwandan Tutsi refugees would later be instrumental in heating up their Burundian counterparts against their Hutu compatriots and would take an essential part both in political assassinations and in the execution of the 1972 genocide. After Burundi's independence on July 1st, 1962, the power of the Tutsi and the segregation of Hutus had continued to rise under the watch of the Tutsi (Ganwa) King Mwambutsa. On March 31, 1964, for instance, the King had dismissed four ministers from the cabinet, all of them Hutus, which led to the resignation of the Hutu Prime Minister Pierre Ngendanumwe and his replacement by a new one, Albin Nyamoya.

On January 7, 1965, the Mwami Mwambutsa had however been obliged to call back Pierre Ngendanumwe to form a new government. Tutsi groups opposed this move and assassinated Ngendanumwe on January 15. In

May of the same year the Hutu won a majority of seats in the Parliament and selected Gervais Nyangoma as their leader. The mwami had however refused to accept him as Prime Minister and had instead appointed a close Tutsi personal friend, Leopold Biha, to that position. This had led to an attempted coup by the Hutu leaders, but the coup had failed. Consequently, all Hutu leaders as well as Hutus newly elected to Parliament including Bamina and Nyangoma, had been killed. Thousands of Hutu were killed in Muramvya province at the hands of government soldiers and radicalised Jeunesses Revolutionnaires Rwagasore, which had been increasingly been used as an instrument of repression against Hutus standing up to claim their civil rights. Many Hutu intellectuals and students were arrested and many of them disappeared without anybody ever seeing them again until today.

The actual run-up to the 1972 had thus started immediately after Micombero had seized power in November 1966. From that time on, most Hutus had been gradually purged from political power and the army through summary executions, which had rendered the government and the military a de facto instrument of an exclusive power in the hands of Tutsi. Between 1968 and 1969, more Hutu army officers were executed by the Tutsi-dominated government and military, which flared more ethnic tensions. In 1969, chief Hutu government members, army officers and other prominent Hutus had been arrested. The radio had announced that a Hutu plot against the government had failed and in December of that year, the Hutu identified by the regime as conspirators had been tried. Twenty-five were sentenced to death, and others were given long prison terms. Twenty-three of them were summarily executed and many more killed without trial.

Between 1970 and 1971, Micombero, a Tutsi Hima from Rutovu in the Bururi province, had also attempted to oust the Tutsi Banyaruguru from power. His security services arrested a number of Banyaruguru ministers and officers, who were subsequently tried on trumped up charges of conspiracy in 1971 and later sentenced to imprisonment or death. Unlike Hutus, who could easily be executed without anybody to defend them, however, the death sentences of the Banyaruguru were commuted to prison terms and the prison sentences reduced due to the threat of civil war between the Tutsi factions.

Despite the visible threat of this violent build-up of the Tutsi political and military monopoly with recurrent violence against Hutu officers, politicians and lower rank officials, it was hardly imaginable that the discrimination would be pushed so far as to spark an all-out campaign for physical elimination of all Hutus in order to crush any form of political competition with them. With the benefit of the hindsight, it is clearly visible that the gradual but relentless purges were all aimed at cutting off any form of potential resistance when the elimination campaign would be unleashed. And when the pogrom was eventually carried out, they had been so well prepared and planned that there was hardly any intellectual Hutu left to tell the story. Part of the opacity around the genocide is therefore also due to the success of its execution and the one-sidedness of the accounts given of it, which allowed the perpetrators to be the ones to tell the story after having succeeded in eliminating any alternative voice. And as an African proverb goes, "As long as the lions don't have their own storytellers, the hunting tales will always glorify the hunters". The present request is therefore also partly an attempt to tell the true story and debunk the myths glorifying those who slaughtered the people of Burundi and managed to get away with it by distorting the narrative of the 1972 genocide against Hutu.

3. Short Summary of this Petition

This petition alleges that before and after 1972, the Government of Burundi systematically violated the fundamental human rights and committed a genocide against Hutus living under its jurisdiction. This petition limits itself to the events that were preparatory to, or were part of the generalised mass killings of Hutus in 1972 by the Micombero regime. Examples of Hutu killings in respect of which a general inference of Genocide against Hutus can be drawn are illustrated in Annexures A and B. Prominent Hutu and moderate Tutsi leaders (see Annexure B) were killed. More than 300000 Hutu civilians were brutally murdered and buried in mass graves. This was gross violation of international law.

Article 3(b) of the Convention on the Prevention and Punishment of the Crime of Genocide Convention (the Genocide Convention) provides that acts of genocide, conspiracy to commit genocide, direct and public incitement to commit genocide, attempt to commit genocide and complicity in genocide shall be punishable.[8] Violations of human rights and genocide are the most contentious issues in the contemporary world. In the aftermath of the horror, devastating and appalling carnage of the Second World War, Member States of the United Nations (UN) undertook radical steps to transform the international legal order, inter alia, "to save succeeding generations from the scourge of war and to reaffirm faith in fundamental human rights". Subsequently, the International Bill of Human Rights were proclaimed and designed, in greater measure, to lay down international human rights norms and standards of conduct and prevent to recurrences of mass killings or genocide.

From the spring to the summer of 1972, the Micombero Tutsi-dominated regime arrested and executed more than 300 000 men and women civilians and military from Hutu ethnic group with the intention to systematically destroy them. Petitioners allege that to-date thousands of

---

8 Convention on the Prevention and Punishment of the Crime of Genocide (hereinafter the Genocide Convention), adopted under Resolution 260 (III) by the United Nations General Assembly, on 9 December 1948.

victims are still forgotten in mass graves. Some of these mass graves have been deliberately hidden beneath the construction of public infrastructure, such as, the Bujumbura Airport, the Regional Institute of Agronomy and Zoo-technique (IRAZ) in Gitega, while a substantial number of corpses were thrown in Lake Tanganyika and in different rivers such as Rusizi.

As a result of the cold-war context of the time and the general lack of interest in the region by the international community back in the time, the perpetrators and their successive Tutsi-dominated regimes have managed to conceal the extent of their horrendous crimes and keep the victims under traumatic conditions, while distorting the narrative of the massacres to make the perpetrator appear as the victims.

The petition alleges further that because they continued to wield exclusive power and influence in Burundi, the masterminds and perpetrators of 1972 genocide against Hutu have never been held accountable or brought to justice. The alleged perpetrators of the genocide against Hutu have been living their lives without worrying about their crimes knowing that no one will ever bring them to justice, given the fact that they never left anyone behind to tell the story. Beside those who passed away without facing justice, those who are still alive have managed to elude justice by "redeeming themselves" through religious pretences without true repentance, claiming they have been transformed into holiness by becoming "born again christians". For example, the then Minister of Foreign Affairs

Arthémon Simbananiye, who is widely perceived to have been the architect of the 1972 genocide against Hutus, has become a guru of a religious sect named "Eglise vivante de Jesus Christ", while others responsible for the Hutu mass killings are living freely, mostly in North America and Europe.[9]

A Tutsi-Hima of the Babanda clan, born in the commune of Matana, in Bururi province, Simbananiye emerged as a leading figure of the so-called Bururi "lobby" in the early 1970s. As Minister of Justice in 1971, he staged the parody of justice that presided over the trial of several high-ranking Tutsi politicians of Banyaruguru origins suspected of monarchist sympathies. Described as a man of "limitless cynicism, ambition and cruelty" (Remarques Africaines, May 1972), Artémon Simbananiye is by and large considered as the principal architect of the mass murders of Hutus in 1972. On the eve of the bloodbath he served as Minister of Foreign Affairs, Cooperation and Planning. It was in this capacity that he negotiated with Idi Amin of Uganda the return of Charles Ndizeye (King Ntare V), a conspiracy that led to his assassination in Gitega on April 29, 1972. Simbananiye's name remains associated in Hutu memory with the "Simbananiye Plan", a Machiavellian plan presumably aimed at killing enough Hutus to ensure numerical parity between Hutus and Tutsis. Although no documented records have been brought to light so far,

---

[9] See Ndayahoze, M. Le Plan Arthemon Simbananiye d'extermination des Hutu : Rapport Politique, Ministere de L'information Cabinet du Ministre, N° 093/100/CAB/68. Avalable at: http://burundi-agnews.org/plansimbananyearthemon.htm (accessed on 8 July, 2014).

the Simbananiye Plan is regularly cited by many Hutus as irrefutable retrospective proof that the genocide of Hutus was planned long before it happened. After his fall from grace in 1987, Simbananiye went into exile, only to return to Burundi a few years later as a Born-Again-Christian.[10]

Hutu survivors of the 1972 killings suffered a mental breakdown. The stress and trauma they went through had left them in an ongoing state of fear and unworthiness. The denied proper burial and proper grieving led to a denied of proper closure of this stressful episode. Today, after so letting them languish in many years of undeserved suffering, it is important to admit that we owe justice not only to the victims and survivors of the 1972 genocide against the Hutu, but to entire humanity. The crime committed in Burundi in 1972 against the Hutu population was a crime against humanity. The perpetrators led by President Michel Micombero were drawn overwhelmingly from minority Tutsi army. Tutsi refugee from Rwanda also played an important role in the execution of the massacres. They mercilessly tortured and killed defenceless innocents Hutu and left no educated Hutu behind to tell the story. We cannot keep our silence any longer and neutrality is not an option. We cannot ignore the crimes committed against Hutu in 1972, unless we have chosen the side of the oppressor.

---

10 See Lemarchand, R. (2008) "Simbananiye Artémon" Online Encyclopaedia of Mass Violence, available at: http://www.massviolence.org/Simbananiye-Artemon.

Petition requests Burundian national institutions as well as the United Nations to mandate a diligent inquiry into the 1972 systematic massacres of Hutu by the Micombero regime, with the view to shed light on the genocide character of these massacres and bring the perpetrators to face justice. Without such an inquiry, the distorted narrative put forward by the perpetrators will continue to dominate the debates about those horrendous crimes, so that the resulting repression of a genuine grieving process will continue to stand in the way of a sincere reconciliation and the desired ethnic harmony in Burundi. Petition requests the Secretary General of the United Nations to deploy all possible efforts to ensure that once the genocidal nature of the massacres is established by the requested inquiry, the many hundreds of thousands of victims and survivors of this genocide be recognized as such and receive the justice, recognition and post-traumatic support they deserve.

4 Facts Underlying this Petition

A. The Mass Killings of Hutus Amounting to a Genocide

The repetitive mass killings of Hutus in Burundi since the assassination of Prince Louis Rwagasore, the father of Burundi's independence, when analysed systematically, appear beyond any reasonable doubt to amount to a genocide. Those massacres targeted Hutu trade unionists, political elites, university students, school children and civilians who were murdered under the Tutsi-led military regimes.[11] Gahutu has elaborated on the persecution and elimination of Hutus and moderate Tutsis in 1961-1965 and during the military regimes from 1966-1993.[12] In particular, the systematic elimination of Hutus from all state institutions, schools and universities gives a compelling account of the nature of preparation, organisation and execution by the Micombero government of a plan aimed at destroying in whole or in part the Hutu ethnic group and rendering it incapable of participating in the national political process. Although Bentley and Southall were unclear as to whether those killing of Hutus amounted to genocide, yet they accept that on the whole, Burundi had endured mass killings bordering on genocide that have gone unpunished.[13] Krueger and

---

[11] For these killings see for example, Lemarchand, R. (1974). Selective Genocide in Burundi, London Minority Group; Kiraranganya, B. (1985). La Vérité sur le Burundi: Sherbrook Editions Naaman: Canada; Ndarubagiye, L. (1995). The Origin of the Hutu-Tutsi Conflict. Nairobi; Leonce Ndarubagiye, Gahutu, R. (2000). Persecution of the Hutu of Burundi. Dar es Salaam: Great Lakes Higher Education Company Limited; Ould-Abdallah, A. (2000). Burundi on the Brink 1993-1995: A UN Special Envoy Reflects on Preventive Diplomacy. United States Institute of Peace Press, Washington D.C., p. 22(Ahmedou Ould-Abdallah was the UN Envoy to Burundi 1993 – 1995 who was sent to stabilize the political situation immediately after the assassination of a Hutu President Ndadaye); Bentley, K.A. and Southall, R. (2005). An African Peace Process: Mandela, South Africa and Burundi: Nelson Mandela Foundation: HSRC Press: CapeTouwn; Ndagijimana, J. (2005) Bujumbura Mon Amour, La Pagaie and Krueger, R. and **Krueger,** K.T. (2007). From Bloodshed to Hope in Burundi: Our Embassy Years During Genocide. University of Texas Press.
12 Gahutu, op cit n. 18 at pp.17- 56.
13 Bentley and Southall, op cit n. 18 at p. 31.

Krueger have stressed that Burundi has had a history of torture and an unhappy legacy of assassinations of leaders and civilians by the Tutsi-led army. [14]

Petitioners maintain that Hutu mass killings of 1972 amount to genocide. Ndagijimana Jean-Marie Vianney, a Rwandan law student at the University of Burundi, who witnessed mass killings of Hutu students at the University premises in 1972, has argued that "There is no need to be a criminal law expert to understand the mass killings in in Burundi amounted to a genocide".[15] The author recalls how government, police and army officials drew up a list of persons belonging to Hutu ethnic group and concludes that this act culminated into the deaths of thousands of civilians, including 700 university students who were murdered within a period of three months in 1972.[16]The testimonies of the way the systematic elimination of hutus from the University of Burundi is illustrative of the generalised nature character of targeted destruction of an entire ethnic group. Similar scenarios took place across the country so that the massacres that started at the end of April, had reached more than 300.00 killed at the end of the summer. According to Ndagijimana, back then a 21-year-old law student in Bujumbura: "On the first day of the raids on the university site, only several hundred Hutu students at the university of Bujumbura campus were sent

---

14 Krueger and Krueger, op cit n. 18, p. 24
[15] Ndagijimana, op. cit. n18, p.62-66
[16] Nagijimana, ibid.

to their last trip. Soldiers will come back the next day, the following day, and every day in May and June 1972 until there was no more Hutu at the University of Burundi. In two months, more than 700 Hutu students were taken under the same conditions, according to the same unchanging scenario, to the camps of death carefully and secretly arranged long before the killings. And I am speaking here only about what happened at the university Bujumbura Campus! None of those arrested on campus ever returned alive after those raids that were clearly premeditated and planned by a government supposed to protect all its citizens. Ndagijimana is still haunted by the atrocious manner in which Hutu students were killed and dumped in mass graves or given to crocodiles and hippos at the Lake Tanganyika.

Ndagijimana, who later became Rwandan Ambassador to France testified: "I do not tell an invented story. I invent nothing. I do not write a novel. I do not give myself to the analysis of situations like the experts. I do not accuse. I testify on what I saw. What I have experienced. In my flesh. I treat my wounds. Deep.wounds that have stood the test of time. Old wounds of 34 years. "(p.4). Coincidence or not, that's when (the Swiss Professor of Political Economy, Jean Bonvin) addresses the chapter on Malthusianism the auditorium door opens with a crash, causing a stir in the room. Armed soldiers, in uniform, led by a young officer flanked by a tall civil in a white shirt, creep into the classroom without deigning to ask permission of the teacher. The plainclothes officer holds in his hand few sheets of paper.

With straight face, the officer ordered us to get out and go in the central courtyard of the University. Professor Bovin advances towards the military and tries to intervene. He asks him what was going on with this muscled intrusion. In response, the young officer aims his weapon against the chest of the Swiss who receding, does not dare raise more protests. Paralyzed by fear, we ran downstairs at full speed. Within seconds, we find ourselves in the central courtyard of the University. Hundreds of other comrades have already accumulated there. Fully armed the military treated them as criminals. The plainclothes officer in a white shirt, accompanied by the young officer, ordered silence in this impromptu meeting. He began to call out names. Dozens of comrades, all Hutus, were invited to come forward and get prone. There, on the dirty warm sand. However, some of them were not called. When the executioner judged the pile of Hutu was enough to fill four military trucks, he ordered the arrested victims to board the trucks. Trucks filled to bursting with bodies, Tutsi students were overjoyed. The first warning that rise is to remain standing. Bluntly, soldiers ordered them to lie face down. Faced with reluctance of some students, soldiers are attacking their victims with rifle butts and bayonets, piercing their helpless young victims as they let out grunts of pain. As my comrades, I cry of fear and disgust at so much hatred and cruelty. But I also cry of rage at the attitude of some Tutsi students who do not hide their joy at the spectacle worthy of another era".

Given the facts mentioned above it is easy to understand why some of the most notorious atrocities occurred on the premises of the University of Bujumbura, secondary and technical schools. A good example is Kiremba Christian High School in Bururi and other High Schools where Hutu students were physically assaulted by their Tutsi classmates and then beaten to death.[17] In a scenario that would repeat itself, groups of soldiers and members of the then ruling party UPRONA youth wing the Jeunesses Révolutionnaires Rwagasore would suddenly appear in classrooms calling Hutu students by names and take them away and these Hutu students never returned back home.[18]

The trucks were already filled with inert bodies piled on each other. The military rise in turn standing on the back of their prisoners. Our poor comrades suffocating under the weight of their executioners. Kicking, bayonets, spittle, insults, nothing was left to chance. When the trucks started, carrying their deadly human cargo, some of our friends were probably already dead. They were smothered, there before our eyes, for nothing, or rather, and because of their ethnicity, nose and size. This went on

---

[17] A focus group interview in, Bujumbura, Gatumba, Gitaza, Rumonge, Tanzania, South Africa in December 2010- January 2011.
18 Ndarubagiye, op cit n. 18 at p. 37.

in all institutions in all universities of the country, in all secondary schools and even in some primary schools. The objective was clear: destroy all the Hutu intellectuals, that is to say those Hutus who had access to formal schooling, from primary school to university, those who, in short, were likely to become leaders one day. This is a GENOCIDE and ought to be called that way. One does not need to be an expert in international criminal law to understand it (p.62-66).

This petition contends that the genocide of Hutus in Burundi can be inferred and interpreted against the background of the Stanton's eight stages of genocide as follows:[19]

- ☐ **Classification**- Burundian community has been categorized into Hutu, Tutsi and Twa ethnic groups whose social, political and economic statuses have been determined according to ethnicity and regional background.

- ☐ **Symbolism**- in Burundi apart from ethnic classification other means of grouping Burundians such as names and symbols have been used to reinforce stereotype and prejudice. For example, "northerners and southerners" or "Bahima and Banyaruguru" [20]or "SP" which stands for a French

---

19   Stanton,   G.H.;   "The   8   Stages   of   Genocide",   available   at: http://www.genocidewatch.org/aboutgenocide/8stagesofgenocide.html.[accessed   on 05/09/2014].

acronym for "Sang Pur" to mean "Pure Blood",[21] implying that Tutsis are inherently superior.[22] In the post-conflict era, other names like "refugees", "returnees" or foreigners" and abasangwa have emerged to supplement these already existing groups and sub-groups.[23]

☐ **Dehumanisation**- in Burundi Tutsis, although the minority, ruled the government and created anti-Hutu sentiments. Hate speeches and propaganda has been used to criticize the Hutu population. For example, an inference can be drawn from the White Paper commonly known as "Plan Simbananiye" issued by the Micombero regime on the eve of 28 April 1972,[24] media reporting during Tutsi military regimes on how to deal with "Abamenja" or "traitors." The "Abamenja" word had been used by Tutsi extremists before and after 1972 to dehumanise they fellow Hutu.

☐ **Organisation**- The Tutsi-led army, militias, security

---

20 Ndarubagiye, ibid at p.xv.

[21] Ndarubagiye, ibid at p.42.

[22] Krueger and Krueger op cit n. 18 at p. 24.

23 Krueger and Krueger op cit n. 18 at p. 24.

24 See Fransen, S.; and Kuschminder, K.; (2012) "Back to the Land: The Long-term Challenges of Refugee Return and Reintegration in Burundi" New Issues in Refugee Research: Research Paper No.242 at pp. 14-15, available at: http://www.unhcr.org/5040ad9e9.pdf [accessed on 15/04/2014]. According to Fransen and Kuschminder returnees are labelled according to the countries they fled to, such as "Tanzanians", "Congolese", "Rwandese", "South Africans" as the list is open-ended.

services, police and gendarmerie were formed, trained and organised to execute their fellow Hutu officials, and civilians in mass murder in order to Kill every Hutu adult and don't live anyone behind to tell the story.[25] Consequently, the Hutu mass killings of 1960s, 1972 occurred pursuant to their extermination plans like the Simbananiye Plan..[26]The aim of this plan was to provoke the Hutus into staging uprisings in order to justify a devastating repression and thus cleanse the country once and for all of the so-called "Hutu peril".[27]

☐ **Polarization** in Burundi, moderates from the Tutsi ethnic group were perceived to have the ability to stop the mass killings, therefore, they became the first victims to be arrested and killed. For example, the assassination of Prince Rwagasore, King Ntare V, and other Tutsi moderates in 1961- 1970s.[28] Tutsi

---

[25] See Céline Cossette in Le Devoir, on 3 October, 1972, who stated that "the Hutu killings of 1972 constitute the culmination of a horrible plan designed by Arthémon Simbananiye, which was found at each stage of repression against the Hutus. It was a "diabolical plan" premeditated in July 1967 to bring the two ethnic groups (Hutus 85% and Tutsis 15%) to number equality. Available at: http://www.burundi-agnews.org/agnews_geno5_1972.htm [accessed on 15/04/2014]. See also International Commission of Inquiry Report for Burundi genocide of 1993.

26 Tutsi army, police, gendarmerie and members of the UPRONA youth wing- JRR in 1972.

27 The Directives of Arthémon Simbananiye, Minister of Foreign Affairs at the time of Hutu mass killings of 1972.

[28] For example the Hutu uprising that resulted into the 1972 genocide. The aim of the Simbananiye plan was presumably to provoke the Hutus into staging an uprising so as to justify a devastating repression and, thus, cleanse the country once and for all of the Hutu threat. See Hoyt Report on Genocide of 1972.

extremists targeted moderate Tutsis in order to silence them and prevent them from any intervention in favour of the targeted Hutu victims.

☐ **Preparation** The 1972 attempt to eliminate the entire Hutu elite came as a culmination of a long strategy that had started at the eve of the independence. The various purges that characterised the political atmosphere of the early post-independence years point to the intention to physically eliminate the Hutus, as they were seen as likely to claim equal rights end proportional representation in the political process, which would have challenged the Tutsi monopoly of political power instituted since the pre-colonial time and consolidated under Belgian colonial administration. The turning point came in 1965, when Hutus of the national gendarmerie attempted coup d'état against the oppressive monarchy regime that was tempering with the election results to deny the Hutus their democratic victory. The failed coup attempt led to a government-sponsored repression in which thirty-eight Hutu officers and non-commissioned officers were executed. Virtually every Hutu leader [in Bujumbura] was apprehended. Eighty-six death sentences were handed down by improvised military tribunals. [29] The impact of this attempted

---

[29] Lemarchand, *Ethnic Conflict and Genocide* 71

coup was immense and resulted not only in the near physical elimination of the entire first generation of Hutu leaders, but also significantly weakened the "government machine built around the royal Court."[30] This weakening of the government allowed the Burundian army, led by Captain Michel Micombero, to overthrow the monarchy and proclaim the first Republic (November 28, 1966). He immediately instituted an intense exclusionary measure in the country, especially in the fields of education and employment and their properties being expropriated. In other words, Hutus and Twas were segregated and discriminated against, directly or indirectly. According to Weinstein (197 6:34), in March 1972, Burundi security and military personnel visited Tanzania to organize surveillance of the Hutu refugees who had lived there in exile since the 1960s. In March also, the former King Ntare was arrested in Bujumbura. On April 16, 1972, there were mass arrests of young and old peasants Hutu in the Nyanza-Lac region Southwestern Burundi. On April 27, the minister of interior Albert Shibura who also served as minister of Justice visited Nyanza-Lac "for a secret meeting" of local Tutsi leaders. Arms were distributed to the local Tutsi officials and government workers. This distribution of weapons to the tutsi on the eve of the slaughter completed the

---

[30] Lemarchand, *Ethnic Conflict and Genocide* 72

process of preparation. The situation needed only a trigger to explode and lead to the next stage, that of extermination.

☐ **Extermination-** at this stage politically- motivated killings begin and quickly become mass killings which in legal terms are referred to as extermination or "genocide". It is "extermination" because the perpetrators do not recognize their victims as complete human beings. When extermination is supported by the state, the armed forces often work with militias to execute the plans. Sometimes genocide results from revenge killings by groups against each other, creating the downward cycle of bilateral genocide. Aware of the Nyaza-Lac meeting, Hutu organized themselves into self-defence group. As had happened in the past, on April 29 a group of Hutus tried to precipitate a revolt against the ruling Tutsi. Though the conflict at first, appeared to be a simple Hutu vs. Tutsi event, the US government was aware from the onset of intra-ethnic tension between northern "moderate" Tutsi faction (i.e. Tutsi Banyaruguru) and southern "radical" Tutsi group (i.e. Tutsi-Hima).[31] It's worth noting that up to this date, most Burundian including Tutsi believe that the Tutsi elite had planned for the Hutus to stage an uprising, so that they would have

---

[31] US Embassy cables, April 29th,1972. Bujumbura 385.

reasons to racially cleanse the country in order to avoid future Hutu revolt. [32] The Micombero regime killed all Hutus, especially the educated, to rule out any future threat of a Hutu rebellion.[33]

☐ **Denial**- denial of genocide always follows after genocide has been committed. It is among unquestionable indicators of further genocide. The perpetrators of genocide dig up the mass graves, burn the bodies, try to conceal evidence and intimidate the witnesses. The perpetrators of genocide deny that they committed any crimes and often tend to shift blame on the victims. In Burundi"s case, there has been denial of genocide in terms of blocking investigations of genocide. For example, Ndarubagiye has claimed that Buyoya staged a second coup d'état in 1996 in order to prevent the future investigations.[34] At the denial stage, perpetrators continue to govern until driven from power by force, when they flee into exile and remain indirectly in power with complete impunity. [35]

Using Stanton's eight stages of genocide in Burundian context, petitioners contend that the first stage of classification which involves the division between ethnic

---

32 See Krueger and Krueger, op cit.p. 11.

[33] Krueger and Krueger, ibid at p. 30 and Ndarubagiye, op cit p. 44.

[34] Ndarubagiye, ibid. at p. 89

[35] Interview conducted in 2010 and 2011, see also Krueger and Krueger, op cit n.18 at p. xiii.

classifications ("us or Tutsis" and "them or Hutus") lays down foundation for the second stage of symbolization to flourish through physical characteristics such as names or symbols that are given or attributed to certain groups. The third stage is dehumanization, whereby the humanity of the group is denied. The Hutu ethnic group was often labelled or called certain derogatory names such as "abamenja" during incitement to genocide. The bodies of the Hutu victims were mutilated to express the denial of their humanity. The fourth stage is organization (sometimes an informal one): it is normally carried out by the state in collaboration with its agents or hate groups, but also varies from culture to culture. The fifth, polarization stage, involves the killing of moderates belonging to the perpetrator's group, to neutralize their ability to stop the extermination process. Stage six is characterized by preparation which includes identification of the victim group by either specific external markings or cards, expropriation of property and forced concentration of the victim group in structures such as extermination camps.

As noted above, mass killings of Hutus had existed before 1972. Yet, the 1972 mass killings bore a particular gravity as they set the stage for other incidents of a genocide dimension, which followed later under the Buyoya regime in 1988 and 1993. During the period of 1962-1965 most Hutu politicians and army officers were killed, and the King refused to appoint a Hutu Prime Minister who won the 1965 elections. A turning point in the escalation of Hutu-Tutsi tensions came in May 1965 with the subversion of the first post-independence elections to the National Assembly.

In 1966, the constitutional monarchy was overthrown by a Tutsi military officer, Micombero, who ruled with an iron fist and carried on with the extermination of Hutus.[36]

Given the Hutu killings of 1962-1965, terror among Burundian was widespread amid rumours of plots and counterplots. It must be pointed out that there were divisions also within the Tutsi ethnic group (the Tutsi-Hima from the south and the Tutsi-Banyaruguru from the north which was perceived by the Micombero regime as threatening. This resulted into arrests and trials of Tutsi Banyaruguru politicians and Hutu elites when they were accused of working hand in hand with the monarchists who wanted to overthrow the Micombero regime. It is common knowledge that the complexities of Burundi issues lie in the fact that power was highly centralized in the hands of a small fraction of the Tutsi minority which viewed itself as power holder and had a distinct social category. [37]

That the massacres of Hutu in 1972 were systematically planned can be inferred from the distribution of weapons to Tutsi in Nyanza-Lac and Rumonge, just prior to the mass slaughter. Those weapons were certainly used in the ensuing orgy of violence. Gahutu has reported that on

---

[36] See Ndarubagiye, op cit n. 18 at p.x.

[37] See Lemarchand, R. (2002) "Le génocide de 1972 au Burundi: Les silences de L„histoire" at pp. 551–67. Cahiers d'Etudes Africaines, No. 167, XLII–3.

the evening of April 27, 1972 the then Interior Minister, Albert Shibura, a Tutsi, arrived at a Tutsi civil servant meeting in Rumonge and stated the following:

> "Brothers, if we look at what happened in Rwanda in 1959, we will see that as the Hutu grew in number they became conceited. The time has therefore come to diminish their number. If you want to save them keep only the illiterate, they aren't any threat to us.[38]

Along with the above statement, Shibura assured the attendees of a plan of action including supplying them with rifles. This was in line with the argument that the Hutu killings were prepared long before in what is commonly referred to as the Simbananiye Plan or the directives of Arthémon Simbananiye.[39] Undeniably, the Simbananiye Plan played a key role in organizing the Hutu who have been marginalized by Tutsi for decades. It is worth noting that up to this date, most Burundians, Hutu, Tutsi and Twa believe that elite Tutsis had discriminated, provoked Hutu and mostly planned for the Hutus to stage an upraise, so that they would have reasons to racially "cleanse" the country in order to avoid future Hutu revolt. The Tutsi ran government under President Micombero, reacted harshly

---

38 Gahutu, op cit n. 18 at p. 56.

[39], Simbananiye cruel plan is reputed to have been aimed at killing enough Hutus to ensure numerical parity between Hutus and Tutsis

and with violent campaigns, against the Hutu majority population. The Burundi army with the help of the virulent most dominantly Tutsi Jeunesses Révolutionnaires Rwangasore (JRR) the youth wing of the Union for National Progress (UPRONA) the ruling party, began detaining Hutu leaders. They were mostly, targeted primarily civil servants, educated males and university students, solely because of their "Hutuness" and irrespective of whether they posed a threat or not.

In the mass killings of 1972, as the social profile of the victims suggests, there was an element of rationality behind such carnage. For instance, the killing of all educated Hutu elites including civil servants, university students, women, elderly persons and schoolchildren amounted to ethnic cleansing. As Lemarchad has contended in respect of the White Paper issued by the Micombero regime, extermination of Hutus was on the agenda.[40] Hutu carnage was carried out in order to prevent any potential of a Hutu rebellion in the foreseeable future.

Genocide is one of the most shocking crimes in the world. The idea of exterminating a part or whole group of people has been part of international humanity's concerns as a call to end genocide have been reinforced in the UN Resolutions[71] and enacting laws like the Genocide, and Torture Conventions.[41] Additionally,

---

40 See Lemarchand, ibid.

the International Criminal Court (ICC) Rome Statute which
compliments the previous UN Conventions attests to the
global commitment to end genocide.[42]
Articles 2 and 3 of the Genocide Convention state that
"genocide means any of the following acts committed
with intent to destroy, in whole or in part, a national,
ethnical, racial or religious group, as such:

a) Killing members of the group;

b) Causing serious bodily or mental harm to members
   of the group;

c) Deliberately inflicting on the group conditions of life
   calculated to bring about its physical destruction in
   whole or in part;

d) Imposing measures intended to prevent births within
   the group;

---

[41] See the United States Supreme Court"s decision in the case of In re Yamashita, 327 U.S.
1 (1946) which held a Japanese general responsible for a pervasive pattern of war crimes
committed by his officials while he knew or should have known that they were going to
commit such crimes but failed to prevent or punish them.

42 See for example, Convention on the Prevention and Punishment, 1948, Convention
Against Torture and Other Cruel, Inhuman or Degrading Treatment or Punishment, 1984.
See the Statute of the International Tribunal for the Prosecution of Persons Responsible
for serious violations of International Humanitarian Law committed in the Territory of the
former Yugoslavia since 1991, UN Security Council Resolution 827/1993 of 25 May 1993,
as amended by Resolutions 1166/1998 of 13 May 1998, Resolution 1329/2000 of 30
November 2000, Resolution 1411/2002 of 17 May 2002 and Resolution 1431/2002 of 14
August 2002; Statute of Rome.

e) Forcibly transferring children of the group to another group."

The Genocide Convention is undeniably considered part of customary international law, as shown in the opinion of the International Court of Justice on the provisions of the Genocide Convention, and as was recalled by the United Nations' Secretary- General in his Report on the establishment of the International Criminal Tribunal for the former Yugoslavia,[74] the International Criminal Tribunal for the Prosecution of Persons Responsible for Genocide and other serious violations of International Humanitarian Law committed in the Territory of Rwanda and Rwandan Citizens Responsible for Genocide and other violations committed in the territory of neighbouring states, between 1 January 1994 and 31 December 1994, the UN Security Council Resolution 955/ 1994 of 8 November 1994 as amended by Resolutions 1165 of 30 April 1998; 1329 of 30 November 2000; Resolution 1411/2002 of 17 May 2002 and 1431 of 14 August 2002. The Special Court for Sierra Leone established in 2002 pursuant to UN Security Council Resolution 1315 of 10 August 2000 to try those who bear the greatest responsibility for the war crimes and crimes against humanity committed in Sierra Leone after 30 November 1996, Resolution adopted by the General Assembly on 27 February 2003, Khmer Rouge Trials (A/RES/57/228) which was adopted on 6 June 2003 after four years of tough negotiations between the UN and the

Royal Government of Cambodia, entered into force the 29 April 2005 and established the Extraordinary Chambers in the Courts of Cambodia to prosecute the crimes committed during the period of Democratic Kampuchea between 1975 and 1979. Resolution 1261 (1999) of 25 August 1999, as amended by Resolutions 1314/ 2000, 1379 /2001 of 20 November 2001, 1460 /2003 of 30 January 2003, and 1539 /2004 of 22 April 2004 and S/RES/1612 (2005) on comprehensive framework for addressing the protection of children affected by armed conflicts.

The global trends have shown that the perpetrators of genocide and other serious international crimes can be prosecuted at the international level if there is unwillingness or lack of capacity to prosecute perpetrators at national level. Thus, the "universal jurisdiction" can be invoked as demonstrated in the cases such as *Pinochet,* [43] *Eichmann*[44] and cases or the ICC"s "complementary principle" can be applied as shown in the *Taylor,*[45] *Kenyatta,*[46] *Ruto,* [47] *Barasa*[48] and *Gaddaffi* [49] cases.

---

43 R v Bow Street Metropolitan Stipendiary Magistrate, Ex Parte Pinochet Ugarte 3.
44 Attorney-General of Israel v Eichmann (1962) 36 I.L.R 5.
45 See Prosecutor v Charles Ghankay Taylor, Case No. SCSL-03-01-A.
46 See The Prosecutor v Francis Kirimi Muthaura and Uhuru Muigai Kenyatta to Trial Chamber V ICC-01/09-02/11- 414.
47 See The Prosecutor v William Samoei Ruto and Joshua Arap Sang Case No. ICC-01/09-01/11 of 29 March 2012
48 See The Prosecutor v Walter Osapiri Barasa Case No. ICC-01/09-01/13.
49 Criminal Court Through its Involvement in Libya" Fordham Law Review, at pp. 2296-2298.

Human rights are fundamental rights that any person has, simply because of being a human being.[50] Human rights are inherent in every human being, hence these rights are universal, inalienable (not transferable) and interdependent.[51] Donnelly has affirmed that human rights are rights that any person deserves because of being a human being,[52] they are inalienable rights no matter how inhumanely people treat or act towards each other.

Bills of Rights which enshrine a list of individual rights that every person is entitled to are mostly adopted by many states that observe the rule of law and democracy. After the atrocities of WWI and WWII for example, many countries in the world came together and proclaimed the Universal Declaration of Human Rights,1948.This human rights instrument was followed by other instruments such as the International Covenant on Civil and Political Rights and the International Covenant on Economic, Social and Cultural Rights, 1966, the African Charter on Human and Peoples' Rights, 1987 (African Charter), Convention on the Elimination of All Forms of Discrimination against Women,1979 (CEDAW), International Convention on the Elimination of All Forms of Racial Discrimination, 1965 (ICEAFRD), International Convention on the Protection of

---

50 See Leanos, B.; (2012) "Cooperative justice: understanding the Future of the International
51 See Alston P. "Making Space for New Human Rights: The Case of Right to Development" Harvard Human Rights Year Book (1988) 3-40, Buergenthal, T.; (1988) International Human Rights in Nutshell. West Publishing Compan. .p. 21.
52 See the Vienna Declaration of 1993 after the World Congress.

the Rights of All Migrant Workers and Members of Their Families,1990 (Migrant Workers Convention), Convention on the Rights of the Child, 1989, Genocide Convention, 1948, Convention against Torture and Other Cruel, Inhuman or Degrading Treatment or Punishment, 1984 (Torture Convention), ICC Rome Statute, 1998 just to mention a few.

There are four international crimes recognizable under international criminal law namely, genocide, crime against humanity, war crimes and aggression whose *actus reus* and *mens rea* elements must be proven. The conduct element in terms of Article 2 of the Genocide Convention includes killing, causing serious bodily or mental harm, deliberately inflicting conditions designed to destroy a particular group; imposing measures to prevent birth and forcibly transferring children of the group to another group.

At national level in contemporary societies, the Constitution aims to ensure the functionality of state organs and their relationship inter-se. In Burundi for example, Title XII of the 2005 Post-transition Constitution of allows for the establishment of, among others, National Councils and National Monitoring Unit (NMU) (*l'Observatoire National*)[53] to uphold the constitutional <u>values through the prohibition</u> of genocide and other

53 Donnelly, J.; (1999) "Human Rights, Democracy and Development" Human Rights Quarterly at p. 611. See Articles 1 and 2 of the UDHR, The Declaration of Tehran, 1986 and the Vienna Declaration, 1993 which reaffirmed the UDHR and the UN Charter. Tehran Declaration, 1986 for example affirms that the civil and political rights cannot be fully realized without realizing the economic, social and cultural rights.

serious international crimes. The NMU is empowered by law[54] to prevent and eradicate genocide, war crimes and crimes against humanity in many aspects including:

- following regularly the development of Barundi community guided by prevention and eradication of the crime of genocide, war crimes and crimes against humanity,

- suggesting effective measures to fight against impunity for crimes committed,

- promoting the creation of regional monitoring unit,

- promoting a national inter-ethnic front of resistance against genocide, war crimes and other crimes against humanity as well as globalization and collective culpability,

- enacting legislation against genocide, war crimes and other crimes and to monitor their strict observance,

- proposing policies and measures for the rehabilitation of victims and

- contributing to the implementation of a large

---

54 Article 268 of the Post-Transition Constitution, 2005. Article 274 of the Constitution, ibid.

sensitisation and education program for peace, unity and national reconciliation.

Article 275 goes further and requires the NMU to prepare and submit an annual report relating to the prevention and eradication of these crimes to the President, Government, the National Assembly and Senate. The law under Articles 268, 274 and 275 of the Constitution clearly reiterates the requirements of the Genocide Convention[55] which, *inter alia*, require the Contracting Parties to prevent and punish the perpetrators of genocide. Thus, the Genocide Convention articulates knotted principles of responsibility to prevent genocide and punish the perpetrators.

Notably, State Parties are under a duty to enact necessary legislation to give effect to the provisions of the Genocide Convention including granting extradition in accordance with their national laws and treaties.

Although the Burundi Constitution of 2005 emphasizes investigating, prosecuting, and the punishing of the perpetrators and the rehabilitation of the victims in a substantive sense, however, the government lacks political will and adequate legal enforcement to investigate and prosecute international crimes committed over 42 years when the 1972 Genocide against Hutus was committed as acknowledged in Protocol I of the Arusha Agreement[56] (see Annexure C).

---

55 Articles I, V, VII of the Genocide Convention
56 Arusha Peace and Reconciliation Agreement of 2000, available at:

4 Violations of International Law

The Burundian Constitution of 2005 requires that international law be considered when dealing with human rights issues and large-scale crimes of the dimensions such as the massacres of Hutus in 1972. [57] Burundi is a signatory to many international human rights instruments which re-enforce the rights enshrined in the Universal Declaration of Human Rights and the International Bill of Rights.

Since 1990, former Heads of States or governments from different countries have been legitimately prosecuted for serious human rights violations, with arguably reparations for the victims. Lessons can be drawn from case studies of high-profile prosecutions of former government officials such as: Augusto Pinochet (Chile), Alberto Fujimori (Peru), Slobodan Milosevic (former Yugoslavia), Charles Taylor (Liberia and Sierra Leone) and Efraín Ríos Montt (Guatemala) just to mention a few. However, the 1972 Burundi human rights violations have gone silent even though the world knew that Hutu were laughter by a Tutsi

---

http://www.issafrica.org/AF/profiles/Burundi/arusha.pdf
[57] See title II of the 2005 Burundi Constitution.

government.

Customary international law and case law as confirmed in the decisions of Municipal Courts, Special Chambers, *ad hoc* International Tribunals, the International Criminal Court (ICC) and International Court of Justice (ICJ) have stressed that (establishing) criminal responsibility (of) and (demanding) accountability to perpetrators are inevitable in order to protect and promote human rights. Thus, the Nuremberg and Tokyo, ICC, International Criminal Tribunal for Yugoslavia (ICTY), International Criminal Tribunal for Rwanda (ICTR), Extra-ordinary Chambers in the Courts of Cambodia (ECCC), Court for Sierra Leone trials, Pinochet and other cases are among the examples that have demonstrated that there can be no immunity for genocide and other serious international crimes.

International criminal law requires specification of the elements of a crime on what must be proven, in other words, material (*actus reus*) and mental (*mens rea*) elements.[47][58] In the case of *Bosnia and Herzegovina v Serbia*, the International Court of Justice emphasized the specific nature of the crime of genocide or specific intent (*dolus specialis*) that targets and destroys an identifiable group in whole or in part is among elements of the crime of genocide.[59] Similarly, the government of Burundi of

---

[58] As Triffterer has clearly articulated, there are subjective elements required to establish criminal responsibility for genocide: the *mens rea* as the pendant to the *actus reus* and the „intent to destroy. See Triffterer, O.; (2001) "Genocide, Its Particular Intent to Destroy in Whole or in Part the Group as Such" Leiden Journal of International Law at p. 400.

1972, identified Hutus as its target group planned, executed and implemented the Simbananiye Plan and other extermination measures in order to destroy in part or in whole the Hutu ethnic group.

Under customary international law for example, rape and other forms of sexual violence are prohibited in both international and non-international armed conflicts. The prohibition of rape under international humanitarian law can be traced way back in the Lieber Code. [60] While Common Article 3 of the Geneva Convention does not explicitly mention rape or other forms of sexual violence. However, it prohibits violence to life and person including cruel treatment, torture and outrages upon personal dignity, which implicitly include rape.[61] The Third Geneva Convention provides that prisoners of war are in all

---

59 See Gill, T.D.; (2007) "The Genocide Case: Reflections on the ICJ"s Decision in Bosnia and Herzegovina v Serbia" Hague Justice Journal at p. 45. Available at: http://www.haguejusticeportal.net/Docs/HJJ-JJH/Vol_2(1)/The_Genocide_Case.pdf

[60] See ICRC "Rule 93 Rape and Other forms of Sexual Violence" available at: http://www.icrc.org/customary-ihl/eng/docs/v1_cha_chapter32_rule93 [accessed on 26/02/2014]. Instructions for the Government of Armies of the United States in the Field (Lieber Code) of 24 April 1863 as prepared during the American Civil War by Professor Francis Lieber and revised and promulgated by President Lincoln. Although they were binding only on the forces of the United States, they correspond to a great extend to the laws and customs of war existing at that time. The Lieber Code has influenced the codification of the laws of war and the adoption of similar regulations by other states. They formed the origin of the project of an international convention on the laws of war presented to the Brussels Conference in 1874 and stimulated the adoption of the Hague Conventions on land warfare of 1899 and 1907 which later influenced the adoption of the Geneva Conventions, 1949. See Schindler, D. and Toman, J.; (1988) The Laws of Armed Conflict. Martinus Nihjoff Publisher at pp. 2-23.

61 Common Article 3 Geneva Conventions, 1949.

circumstances entitled to respect for their honour and dignity.[62]The prohibition of crimes against personal dignity is acknowledged in the Additional Protocols I and II as a fundamental guarantee for civilians and persons *out of combat zones.*[63]

The crimes listed under the ICC Rome Statute have been confirmed by the international tribunals with specific reference to rape as a crime against humanity under the ICTY and ICTR Statutes and has been interpreted broadly to mean genocide.[64] The ICC Rome Statute obliges the ICC Prosecutor to investigate allegations of genocide if it is clear that the crime was either committed by a national of a State Party or on the territory of a State Party.[65] Articles 12 and 13 of the ICC Statute refer to the conditions relating to the ICC"s jurisdiction to deal with genocide cases including referrals of one state against another State Party. As demonstrated in the UN Report of 2010 commonly known as "the UN Report on Second Rwanda Genocide", there is an indication that gross human rights violations may no longer be concealed.[66]

---

62 Article 14 (1) of the Third Geneva Convention, 1949.

63 See Article 75(2) of Additional Protocol I and Article 4(2) of Additional Protocol II

64 Article 5(g) of the ICTY Statute and Article 3(g) of the ICTR Statute. See also the ICTR judgment in the case of Prosecutor v Akayesu Case ICTR 96-4-T, Judgment 732 (2 September 1998).

[65] Article 13(a) and (c) of the ICC Rome Statute.

66 Fisher, M.; (2010) "UN Report on Rwanda Genocide Shakes Africa" The Atlantic Wire Aug

29, 2010. Available at: http://www.theatlanticwire.com/global/2010/08/un-report-on-rwanda- genocide-shakes-africa/23224/. See also Human Rights Watch "DR Congo UN Report Exposes Grave Crimes: International Efforts Needed to Create Mechanisms to Ensure Justice" October 1, 2010. Available at: http://www.hrw.org/news/2010/10/01/dr-

5 A Call for Recognition

The Hutu mass killings have largely been overshadowed in public memory and more attention have been paid to the devastating 1994 Rwandan bloodbath in the African Great Lakes. The repression and carnage that took place in Burundi in 1972 was qualified undeniably as a "selective genocide".[67] Whitaker Report also characterised the 1972 massacres as a genocide.[68] Taking into consideration the fact that the Tutsi-dominated government executed, across Burundi, all educated Hutu citizens who were able to read and write (this included public servants, businessmen and women, priests, teachers, primary and secondary school learners, university students and other Hutu civilians), these killings amount to a genocide

congo-un-report-exposes-grave- crimes. See further, the case of DRC v Burundi, Rwanda and Uganda, 2004, ACHPR 19, at para 94; Armed Activities on the Territory of the DRC, Order of 21 October 1999, ICJ Reports, 1999 101.

67 See Melady, T. P. Burundi: The Tragic Years (1974). Thomas Patrick Melady was a former American Ambassador to Burundi and Lemarchand, R. and Martin D.; (1974) Selective Genocide in Burundi. London: Minority Rights Group.

68 See the Ruhashyankiko Report, 1978and Whitaker Report, 1985 which have been viewed as the UN Commission on Human Rights" major documents on genocide. Both Reports focus on studies of genocide from the viewpoint of the Sub-Commission on Promotion and Protection of Human Rights and Prevention of Discrimination and Protection of Minorities. The Whitaker Report was intended to correct Ruhashyankiko Report. The Ruhashyankiko Report was construed under political pressure to omit Armenian genocide, but later on the Whitaker Report confirmed that the Armenian massacres amounted to genocide. Whitaker Report elaborates further that Nazi ethnic cleansing has not been the only case of genocide in the twentieth century.

because they were systematically planned and executed by the Government of Burundi. In Burundi, least every Hutu family or household has been negatively affected by the mass killings of 1960s and 1972.[69]

Micombero and his acolytes never were brought to justice. The world owes justice to the victims and the survivors of these horrendous crimes. Their blood is crying for justice while many of the perpetrators are still roaming free.

The term "genocide" was used in the Whitaker Report to refer to the massacres of Hutu civilians in 1972.[70] The Whitaker Report compared and elaborated that Nazi ethnic cleansing of Jewish population has not been the only case of genocide in the twentieth century. It cited other examples of genocide cases such as the German massacre of Hereros in 1904, the Ottoman massacre of Armenians in 1915-1916, the Ukrainian extermination of Jews in 1919, the Tutsi army massacre of Hutus in Burundi in 1965 and 1972, the Paraguayan massacre of Ache Indians prior to 1974, the Khmer Rouge massacre in Kampuchea between 1975 and 1978.[71]

Michael Hoyt, Deputy Chief of Mission from the U.S. Embassy in Burundi at the time of the horrific massacres reported in the following examples of events

---

69 Hoyt Report on Genocide of 1972.
70 Whitaker Report, paragraph 24.
71 Whitaker Report paras.24 and 36.

characterising the 1972 Genocide against Hutus:[72]

> "No respite no let up. What is apparently happening is genocide that continues. Arrests going on around the clock.[73]

> Tutsi reprisals unabated in the interior but have slackened somewhat in Bujumbura. In the north, Hutu take cover upon arrival of any vehicle, reflecting pervasive fear.[74]

> In two days following July 14, three new ditches filled with Hutu bodies near Bujumbura airport. Arrests have continued throughout the week in Bujumbura, in the hills around town, in Ngozi region and central Burundi.[75]

Repression against Hutu is not simply one of killing. It is also an attempt to remove them from access to employment, property, education and the general chance to improve themselves."[76]

A social worker and nurse, Celine Cossette, who stayed in Burundi between 1968 and 1972, commented on the genocide committed against Hutu and the silence of

---

72 See Hoyt Report on Genocide of 1972.
73 Hoyt Report of 26 May, 1972.
74 Hoyt Report of 11 July, 1972.
75 Hoyt Report of 21 July, 1972.
76 Hoyt Report of 25 July, 1972.

public opinion in this regard. The following is what she wrote in October 1972:

"...according to our sources, the killing would have been 200,000 deaths and constitutes the horrible culmination of a plan devised by Colonel Micombero's Minister, Mr. Arthemon Simbananiye, found at every stage of repression against the Hutus. A diabolic plan, masterminded in July 1967, to bring the two ethnic groups (Tutsi 15% and Hutus 85%) to numerical equality" [77]

As Lemarchand has deplored, "nowhere in Africa have human rights been violated on a massive scale and with such brutal consistency than in Burundi".[78] The world, including the United Nations, did nothing, but silently watched while innocents Hutus were being slaughter by the Tutsi elites.

It's worth recalling that the systematic mass killings and unfair discrimination against Hutu population in Burundi are not isolated or founded on one incident. In the

---

[77] Céline Cossette in Le Devoir on 3 October, 1972 who stated that "the Hutu killings of 1972 constitute the culmination of a horrible plan designed by Arthémon Simbananiye which was found at each stage of repression against the Hutus. It was a "diabolical plan" premeditated in July 1967 to bring the two ethnic groups (Hutus 85% and Tutsis 15%) to numerical equality. Available at: http://www.burundi-agnews.org/agnews_geno5_1972.htm [accessed on 15/04/2014]. See also Commission of Inquiry Report for Burundi genocide of 1993 at par. [493].

[78] René Lemarchand's assertion in a testimony to the United States Congress in 1988 on the scale of human rights violations and enduring nature of the cycle of violence in Burundi.

aftermath of the Hutu killings of 1965, which were followed by the Micombero's coup of 1966, were all associated with terror, repression and carnage which culminated into the 1972 Genocide against Hutus. Hutus were summarily executed, tortured, arbitrarily detained and subjected to forced disappearances, while survivors were forced into exile and became refugees in the neighbouring countries, further in Africa or even in other continents. The mass killings of Hutus have been perceived as a tragedy that has negatively affected not only Burundi, but also the countries that have hosted Burundian refugees.[79] Rwegasira has rightly observed that refugee problems in the Great Lakes Region are rooted in politics rather than humanitarian factors.[80] There are now thousands of Hutu survivors of the 1972 mass killings, who eventually found a new home in countries such as Tanzania, the Democratic Republic of Congo (DRC) and other African countries, but also in North America, Europe, Canada, USA, Europe, Australia and the rest of world.

Petitioners allege and stress that it is saddening and disappointing that fourty two years later, the 1972 Genocide against Hutus in Burundi remains

---

79 Brahim, J.; "How Tanzania was Affected by Refugee Crisis in the Great Lakes Region and Her Response to It" in Bunting, I.; and Ngonzi, K.; (ed) (1995) Summary Report From the International Workshop on Refugee Crisis in the Great Lakes Region, East African Oxfam at p.7, available at: http://repository.forcedmigration.org/show_metadata.jsp?pid=fmo%3A1461 [accessed on 08/01/2013].
80 Rwegasira, J.; "An Opening Address: International Workshop on Refugee Crisis in the Great Lakes Region" in Bunting and Ngonzi ibid. at p. 4.

unacknowledged in the eyes of international community. Governments in the world have allowed the persistence of this deep silence, which allows the perpetrators of Genocide against Hutus, war crimes, crimes against humanity and aggression, to travel freely or live peacefully in democratic countries, including Canada, the USA and Europe where they continue to harass and traumatize Hutu survivors who fled the genocide to establish new homes in the same countries[81] (see Annexure C). As a consequence of the continued lack of recognition and the resulting impunity of the perpetrators, hate speech and denial of the committed crimes have been allowed to perpetuate the frustration and traumatism of the victims. For example, Emmanuel Nkurunziza, a nephew of an ex Burundi Commander Officer Samuel Nduwingoma, who was in 1972, the Governor of Bururi Province and was very actively involved in the 1972 Hutu mass killings, wrote a thesis denying that in 1972 as a PhD student at York University, in Toronto, Ontario. His wife, Alice Simbananiye, daughter of the infamous Artemon Simbananiye, and their fellow Tutsi comrades have been accused of being responsible for the June 1995 massacre of Hutu students at the University of Bujumbura Campus. There are many more Tutsi extremists who share Emmanuel Nkurunziza ideology and behaviour, such as Alphonse Kadege, the prominent member of the UPRONA ruling party in 1972, who currently

---

81 See Cotler I, "Victimes au Burundi " Le Courrier Le Devoir, lundi, 18 décembre 1989.

resides in Texas and continue to harass and traumatize Hutu living in the United States.

Petitioners request that the Burundian state institutions and the secretary General of the United Nations undertake the steps leading to a legal recognition of the 1972 Burundi massacres of Hutus as a genocide. Further, petitioners request that action be taken to bring the cycle of impunity of the perpetrators and their denying descendants to an end by bring the perpetrators to justice and making accountable those who perpetuate the traumatism of the victims by denial and hate speech.

Having been obstructed in the attempts to obtain justice from Burundian justice system, petitioners appeal to the United Nations Human Rights Council, requesting the recognition of 1972 Genocide against Hutus and demand that the Government of Burundi of 1972 be held accountable and responsible for the genocide committed against Hutu ethnic group and other grave human rights violations.

According to Resolution 1 (XXIV) of the Sub-Commission on Prevention of Discrimination and Protection of Minorities, exhaustion of domestic remedies is not required if it appears that such remedies would be ineffective or unreasonably prolonged. In this case, no effective domestic remedies are available to the petitioners. Notably, the successive Tutsi-led military regimes of Jean-Baptiste Bagaza (1976-1987) and Pierre´ Buyoya (1987-1993 and 1996-2003) failed to investigate and prosecute the perpetrators of 1972 genocide. The various governments of Burundi have instead made every effort to hinder attempts of the survivors to obtain justice, including harassing and traumatizing them. As a result, survivors and victims' of 1972 genocide live in constant danger and fear inside and outside Burundi.

CHAP IV: TESTIMONIES ON THE 1972 GENOCIDE

TESTIMONY 1: ROSE NDAYAHOZE

Mrs Rose Ndayahoze, a former Burundian citizen and currently Canadian citizen since 1984, is a widow of Captain Martin Ndayahoze, who was among the first victims of 1972 genocide. Martin Ndayahoze served the government of Burundi for six years as a Minister of Information and Economic. He was also a Secretary General of the then ruling UPRONA Party. Martin Ndayahoze warned President Michel Micombero of the plan of Genocide against Hutus and its future implications for the Graet Lakes Region of Africa. He was brutally killed in 1972. With the assistance of the United Nations High Commission for Refugees (UNHCR), in 1981, Mrs Rose Ndayahoze became a refugee in Canada in 1981. In spite of her circumstances as a widow and mother of six children, Mrs Rose Ndayahoze has been under constant attacks, traumatized and harassed by the former ambassador of Burundi to Canada, while some of her husband's assassins like Charles Bitariho (Minister of Health), who took Martin Ndayahoze's car, have subsequently been killed in order to conceal evidence.

TESTIMONY 2: GENEROSE NZOHABONA ON DISAPPEARANCE OF MR. NZOHABONA ANTOINE, BRUXELLES, 22 AUGUST, 2013

Mr. Nzohabona Antoine, my Father, Hutu, was born in 1931 at Kabuye, in Bugendana-Gitega. He studied at Mugera and at "Groupe Scholaire d'Astrida, in agronomic sciences section", then he worked for the Burundian government from
1955 till the 2nd of May 1972 when he was abducted. He married my mother, Tutsi, in 1956 and they had together three daughters and six sons (I was the eldest, born in 1957). Before the Burundian independence, he co-founded the Parti du Peuple as Vice Chairman. In February 1961, he was appointed as Secretary of State for Medical Affairs to the Ministry of Social Affairs by the Secretary General of Ruanda-Urundi, acting on behalf of the Resident-general. In 1965 he was

working as "agronome forrestier" at Bururi. He also acted as "Sénateur Titulaires Suppléant". Three days before Easter, he was warned that the "gendarmes" who were on their way to kill him; he escaped and fled to Bugendana. A lot of his friends, intellectual and politicians were killed and he swore that he will never do politics, that it was time to take care of his family only by doing the job that he had studied for and he kept his promise. From 1968, he was working as "Agronome Forestier" in Bujumbura and we were living in a government rented house at "Fond d'avance". On the 30th April 1972, he was asked by many people to flee because all the Intellectual Hutus were targeted by the government to be killed. He told to all his friends that he had not anymore something to do with politics and that those who were feeling guilty could flee. He was kidnapped outside our home in a car belonging to the National Intelligence Service on the 2nd of May 1972 (at least an eyewitness is still alive). Leaving behind a six months pregnant widow and eight orphans. A few days later, my Mum was told that he has deserted from his job and she was summoned to immediately go out the house. We had to move to an unfinished house that my Dad was building. We had no more right to the health care and other benefits. Without any news, except what people were saying about how the "abamenja" were *tortured before being killed and their bodies taken like small fish and thrown somewhere like rubbish. As any humans who have lost their loved ones, we were not allowed to cry, to mourn or to talk about him in front of people. They did not kill my Father, they have killed all the family (emotionally, socially and financially). My Mum has never been at school and could not get any paid job. At the age of 15, I replaced my father helping my mum to take care of all the family. Our small Volkswagen has been taken, without money to pay a taxi, I witnessed the birth of the latest brother in the road (he has been namedNyanzira because of that). Despite my Mum's and dad's families help, all the kids could not reach our dad's dream, we could not study as he wished, and our lives did not turn out the way he dreamed.*

Besides that, I still do not believe in his death, unless somebody tells me that he has seen his dead body, which is very stressful for me. I have been silently mourning and crying for 42 years. I wish somebody can tell me what really happened to him and where his body is. I wish to have a place to put flowers and I wish justice to be done for his murderers.

TESTIMONY 3: FREDERIC NZEYIMANA TESTIMONY ON KILLING OF HIS FATHER

Summary

Frederic Nzeyimana is a Canadian citizen of Burundi origin. Married and father of three children, he presently lives in the city of Toronto in Canada. Frederic's father,

Terence NDIMBANE, was a teacher at Musongati elementary school, where they lived, in the Province of Rutana. The story of his death is similar to that of many others. He was invited to a business men's' meeting and never returned from it.

Testimony

"I was 11 years and in grade 5 when, on a May 1972 morning, the Provincial School Supervisor came at our school and invited all teachers to a meeting with him at the City Hall. Six teachers for six classes. Four teachers were Hutu. My dad, Romano, Charles and

Venerand Mpfanahasi. The two others were Tutsi-. Ntama Justin and Theodore. Classes were dismissed for the rest of the day. Days passed, and one of the two Tutsi teachers, Justin Ntama, came back to speak with my mother. He said that the meeting was still going on and that my father had requested that he brings him his bicycle and his new suits. Later on, the two Tutsi teachers returned from the meeting. But, none of the four Hutu teachers returned. All have been killed. Until today no one has told us what happened to them. Their bank accounts, salaries were ceased, and their descendants never got anything from the government.

TESTIMONY 4: JEAN MARIE NTAHONKIRIYE TESTIMONY ON KILLING OF HIS FATHER

Summary

Jean Marie Ntahonkiriye is a Burundian living in Australia. His father, Gabriel NTAHONKIRIYE, was a wealthy business man. His successful business and being married to a Tutsi resulted in him being in a circle of "friends" who were mostly if not all Tutsis. Obviously, many of these so-called friends were interested in his wealth than anything else. In April 1972 they had just moved to Bitare (Zone Bitare, commune Bugendana) where his father had built their new family house and was extending his business. Given the respect he had among local people, his father arrest did not take place as they did for other Hutus who were brutalized, beaten up and pushed into back of tracks that were transporting hundreds of them to be killed and thrown into the mass graves.

The dark memory of a six year-old boy

This is just a testimony of the events as lived by a six Years old boy and his family and the subsequent suffering and trauma they have had to carry in silence up to this day. It has not been easy for me to reach this point where I can share my family story simply because I have found myself and my family lost between two ethnic groups, the Hutu and the Tutsi. Therefore, my aim is not to condemn or justify any ethnic group; my testimony is given in the hope that the memory of the Hutu killed just for being Hutu in the dark period of 1972 will be honoured and those responsible for their killing brought to justice. My hope is not limited to seeing the rehabilitation of the victims of 1972 in

Burundi; it extends to all the victims of ethnic cleansing all over the world. Genocide should be condemned and the responsible brought to justice regardless of where it occurs, when it occurs, who is the victim or who is responsible.

Testimony

My name is Jean-Marie Ntahonkiriye, known as Nzungu from my childhood apparently because I was born with a very light skin. I was born in April 1966. Although my birth took place at the Clinique Prince Louis Rwagasore in Bujumbura, my parent residence was in Magarama Gitega were I spent my early childhood. My parents were known as Ntahonkiriye Gabriel (Mukama) and Ntatyora Louise. My father was a Hutu and my mother was a Tutsi. My father was a wealthy businessman. His successful business and being married to a Tutsi resulted in him being in a circle of "friends" who were mostly if not all Tutsis. Obviously, many of these so-called friends were interested in his wealth than anything else.

His circle of friends not only extended to businessmen and people in the position of authority but also people known as the elite class in that time such as those known as being of "Abaganwa" family. I still remember many of the parties at different occasions such as birthday, baptism and communions where we gathered and played together with other kids from these families. Among my father friends was Nzikobanyanka Simon known as "Mwaro" and I believe he was given that name because he came from Mwaro but he lived in Gitega Nyamugari (known as Mugiswahili). He is one of those I could count among my father's closest friends.

In April 1972 we had just moved to Bitare (Zone Bitare, commune Bugendana) were my father had built our new family house and was extending his business there. Among our neighbors was the family of "Bishariza Germain" son of "Mboneko" known as Muganwa. The friendship that developed between us and Bishariza family continued to this day. Some of the administrative authorities were: Barambona Wenseslas (Commissaire de Mutaho), Ntibandetse (Judge de Bugendana), Fanagari Gaspard (Chef de Zone Bitare). Some of the other business men at the centre (Bitare) were of Congolese and Arabs origin.

Prior to my father's arrest

Few days leading to my father being arrested, he seemed very worried. Some of his friends had advised him that given what was happening, there was a possibility that he could be arrested and there was not much they could do to protect him. They suggested that he should flee. Like many other innocents Hutus, he did not flee. However, he had withdrawn a large sum of money which he gave to my mother to look after us , should anything happen to *him.*

The day my father was taken away

Given the respect he had among local people, my father arrest did not take place as they did for other Hutus who were brutalized, beaten up and pushed into back of trucks that were transporting hundreds of them to be killed and thrown into the mass graves. I remember the truck that took him; they came home and told my father that he needs to present himself to the Authority in Gitega for questioning. The driver of that truck was named s Gahutu. They wanted him to go on his own in his own car, however he refused. He requested to go with them instead and they agreed. Maybe going with them gave him some sort of assurance that nothing will happen to him. He was seating in the front seat when they left and that was the last time we saw him. When they came back without my father and asked my mother to give them the key of the car, we then realized that the reason they wanted him to go on his own and in his own car was because they wanted both my father and his car. My mother told them that she did not know where the car keys were. They harassed my mother for a while and when they failed to get the key, they called one of the Arab whose name was "Amer" to come and help them start the car engine.
He came and helped to start the car by braking into the ignition switch, then used the wires to start the engine.

They took the car as well and that was the last time we saw it. My mother was still hoping that our father may come back and this hope faded away when one of my father's friend I mentioned earlier, Nzikobanyanka

Simon (Mwaro) came and said that they tried their best to defend him before the authority saying that he was innocent, but they did not succeed. From that time, we started sleeping in a common room with tremendous fear that they may come after the entire family. As a kid, I really had not grasped what was going on other than noticing that the entire family was scared. My mother was crying all the time, our friends had disappeared all of the sudden.

After my father was taken away

Most of the motive in arresting my father was to take hold of his wealth, in the process they took our home which was in Gitega, Magarama. They took the car and then they went to take the money from my father's bank account and that is when they realized that he had withdrawn a large sum of money as I have mentioned earlier. This led them to come back at our home asking my mother to hand over the money my father had withdrawn from his bank account.

My mother obviously said that my father had not given her any money. At that time, being a kid, I was playing in the backyard with few kids who were still coming around our house. All of the sudden another kid came running shouting to me "Your mum is being taken away". I quickly run at the front of the house in time to notice two men pushing my mother into the back seat of a little white Renault 4, while Barambona Wenseslas (Commissaire de Mutaho) stood by watching on as if nothing was happening. As the car drove off, I run after the car crying and calling mum, mum till I could no longer see the car. I kept on running following after the car I could no longer see and still calling mum, mum.... Somehow, by God grace, Barambona Wenseslas (Commissaire de Mutaho) left, passed me in his car, and minutes later while I was still running, I saw the same car coming back followed by Barambona Wenseslas's car. I could see my mother crying in the back seat of the white car surrounded by the two men I had seen pushing her in the car. I then returned home still running after the car and when I got home my mother was being pushed around in the living room. From the living room to the bedrooms, they put everything in the house upside down. They kept on asking my mother to give them the money. My mother did not give in and all that time I was holding to my mother's cloths while we were both being kicked and pushed around. They finally left and that is when for the first time, I was scared. I cannot express the anger and hatred I felt for these men and I did carry this anger and hatred for so many Years. My father's sister was killed as well during the same period and I never had a chance to know her. Among us, my eldest sister was the most affected as she was old enough to better understand what was going on and she ended up leaving school because she was pointed all the time as being the daughter of "Umumenja" as they called all Hutus killed that time. I remember one day while we were walking from school, another kid from my school came to me and said: "Your father was such a strong man; people said that it took seven bullets to get him to fall down". I was so shocked to not know what to say but those comments stay in your memory forever.

The dog has not died. (Imbwa ntiyapfuye).

Another comment that came to revive our pain came from a man known as Ntibandetse (Judge de Bugendana). It was a Wednesday, a day I went to visit home and I had borrowed a friend's car just for this visit. When Ntibandetse saw me leaving in that car, people who were there reported to my mother what he said as:

"imbwa ntiyapfuye"; which literally means "the dog has not died", in other words, although they have killed my father, he is still alive through his children and they regret to have left his children alive. I tried to find these people I have listed above who were part of the administrative authority during that period; unfortunately they have all passed away. Our trust that our testimonies will allow other people to come forwards and share what they have seen and *may be one day justice will be done.*

TESTIMONY 5: JEAN NDAYIZIGIYE ON MASS KILLINGS STUDENTS (*Seeds for Communities of Peace, USA)*

Testimonies of 1972

The tension has been overwhelming the previous days with students being arrested at the public schools, especially at Athenee de Bujumbura. Arrest of Hutu students: On May 18, 1972 around 10 a.m., the army arrested more than 127 Hutu students from 14th grade (4eme Normale) to 10th grade at "Ecole Normale de L'Etat" of Bujumbura.

After the breakfast, the students gathered, as usual, at the playground to sing the national anthem and salute the national flag. Then, class by class, students followed the instructor for the first class. That morning, our French professor didn't show up. We were told to go directly to class and wait for him. Ten minutes, fifteen, twenty-five minutes passed. He didn't show up. We started to wonder what could have happened to him, normally he was in time. The class delegate went to the principal's office to inquire about what we should do.

After several minutes he came back with the principal,

who advised us to just wait, and eventually review the lessons of the previous day. There was already brouhaha of rolling military trucks in the school compound. We could hear them from our class room. The class delegate told us that he had seen military in every corner inside the school compound. Facing uncertainty, we became nervous, but we stayed calm.

At the end of the first period, we were expecting the instructor of Kirundi. He did not show up. It became more and more scary. However, we stayed calm. We had not seen him the last four days. What had happened to him? We could also see that the non-boarding students were absent. That was not a good sign.

The principal made a tour of all classrooms to tell students that there would be a government communication in a few minutes. He did not take any question. As a European he could barely hide his emotion, his face was red, we could sense his nervousness. We could not know what was behind the announcement, but we guessed something major was going to happen because normally the announcements were written and posted on the office board.

That morning, there was no break between classes, no recreation at 10:00 am. Instead we were told to stay in class and not to move. Nobody dared to ask to go even to the bathroom. Looking through the classroom window outside there were many militaries in the position of attack. The silence was heavy. But we had seen some premonitory signs. Three Hutu professors had not showed up for the last four days. The European professors, who usually chatted with students, had been very quiet, avoiding conversation with the students. Some classrooms such laboratories of chemistry and physics were cancelled and postponed; the room for sports and physical exercises was locked. There was already a state of siege at school. In my class, the 11th grade five students were arrested. We saw. I saw 12 arrested from the 10th grade.

Exactly at 10:35 am, a commander officer accompanied by several military came into our classroom and began to give us the ground rules: "I have a list of students in your class. There is very important information for them, keep quiet until you hear your name. Then stand up and get out. For security reason, every student called will be escorted by military up to the principal office where he will get the information, and then he will be escorted to the dining hall where he will be waiting for his classmates for lunch. Is it clear? I repeat. Don't hesitate to ask questions. But don't make me waste my time by asking stupid questions. Understood? Now let us proceed: N. Boniface, N. Ruben, S. Astere, N. Macaire, Mr. Leandre. In my class, five names were called upon for that important information at the principal's office.

There was consternation for the Hutu and joy for some of the Tutsi students. This visit was unusual; we could see from the windows many soldiers escorted students from other classrooms. We could guess some terrible thing was going to happen to those fellow students.

The commander then went to the tenth grades. We saw ten students being escorted by military. Among them were a famous basketball player and an athletic man who had won many medals and trophies for the school: B. J. Berchmans and M. Calliste. Almost all the Hutu students from the superior cycle (from the 11th grade to fourteenth grade), some of the inferior cycle (eighth grade to tenth grade) were arrested by the army and taken to an unknown destination.

From the classroom, we could hear rolling trucks and painful cries in the playground. We guessed that the students called were submitted to atrocious treatments and tortures. In fact, they received a bayonet coup before they were thrown and packed like sardines in the military trucks. When it was lunch time, we found the military busy cleaning the way from the principal office to the parking lots. We could see traces of blood. Beating the Hutu student, the view of military was terrifying and traumatizing. The Tutsi trivialized to humiliate and terrorize me and the other Hutu who had not been arrested.

In the afternoon, students were allowed to stay on the playground or in the room for information, it was not normal. Tutsi students immediately began grouping around 3:00 pm after signal was given by three "sifflets" (=whistle sounds). Back from the toilet, a group of ten Tutsi classmates armed of sticks (metal and or wood) surrounded and immobilized me. I barely understood the questions they asked me. They assumed I knew something and did not tell them. Their ground rules were that I had to answer to all the questions. For any "no responses" the five students had the right to beat me wherever it fit on my body. For unclear response half of the group had to beat me on. For an escaping response the person who had asked the question had to beat me on the head with his wooden or metallic stick. He could also ask two or three students to beat me wherever it fit for them on my body. There was never any response that could satisfy them, because I did not know anything about the events. They did not trust me. So, I was beaten all the time.

My cry did not mean anything to them. Sometimes I was wondering if I was dealing with human beings or animals. Those were the students we had been together the four last school years, now torturing me. Those were students who during the break, some of them had come to spend the time at my home. I have been to many of their homes. Those were students who went with me to church every Sunday. Three of them were with me in the church choir. Two others were with me on the school basketball team. We played together at the basket team. Most of them had spent nights at my home. I had been to most of their homes. Two of them were sponsored by my brother, Yves. They came to my brother's house as if it was their home. They were always welcome.

Before the exams I was tutoring those, who had some problems especially in mathematics, chemistry, physics, English, French etc…I could never imagine how one could become so ferocious overnight.

I remember, they tore my clothes, except my underwear;

they took away my shoes; then they made me lie down on basketball field; they tied up my hands behind my back, the tiles were very hot. When I began to cry, an erudite student brought water and poured it on me. They pulled me on the tiles ten meters, saying, "Pretend you are swimming in a river". It hurt a lot. The skin was getting torn many places on my chest, abdomen, thighs and knees area and my belly began to bleed. M. Elie had the crazy idea to bring sand and put it on my wounds as to stop the bleeding. N. Gerard had mercy and asked his friends to put on my torn clothes, but S. Lucien refused. Instead they used them to tie more my hands on behind my back.

After the ordeal, they took me from group to group to be questioned. They said: "Here is the cleverest student we have known in our class; he should be able to answer all the questions as he did in the national geographic and history contest." They started with stupid questions connecting me with the "rebel groups", but I did not answer to any of them. Answering or not would not change my fate. They continued to beat me some with bar hands, others with wooden sticks, and iron bars.

After a while they took me to a place where they had dug a hole in the ground, they poured some water in the hole, obliged me to lie down on it pointing my penis in the hole. They told me that they were going to relax me a little bit. H.Philippe told me: "Pretend you are making love in the hole, imagine you are with a beautiful young lady and are making love." I resisted with all the remaining *energy and refused to do what they wanted me to do. They then immobilized me; they tied my legs with my torn clothes. One of them pulled out my penis and pushed it in the hole. He told me:*

"Pretend you are making love and feel happy; this is your last day."

This did not work anyway. They had to invent something else. Then they took me to the soccer field between the dormitory and the Copico military camp. I could see many other Tutsi groupings torturing other Hutu students. It seemed to me that it was something very well-organized and coordinated. They removed my remaining underwear; I was completely naked. Then they began to shave my head with a piece of bottle. They were pouring cold water on the shaved part of my head. It was very painful. They would cut the skin to make me bleed. Then, they would add salted pilipili on the cut to increase the suffering. Finally, they pushed me around, insulting me, calling me by all the names. We made together with my torturers the tour of the soccer field.

I remembered K. Salvator telling me: "Jean you have been the smartest student our normal school had known, during the four years you had spent here, you grabbed all the rewards, all the prizes but gymnastic and civic which were insignificant courses. Now it is time to call upon your intelligence to get you out of this mess, also know that is your last day on earth".

The military that were around, pretending to secure the campus, seemed to enjoy the tortures performed on the

Hutu students by their classmate Tutsi. Surrounded by my torturers and completely naked, I made a tour of the soccer field. Approaching the exit of the soccer, they clothed me with weaved leaves as to replace my clothes and took me to the entrance of the dormitory where I was subjected to more intense interrogatory and tortures. I was bleeding everywhere on my body and so weak that I could not stand up for a while. They had to hold me to keep me standing up.

Around 5:00 pm, two senior students, my best friends, came to the place I was being tortured. They were angry with my classmates who have been torturing me the whole afternoon. Since they were the executive members of the student government association, they were very influential. They ordered my classmates to stop the tortures. Then they took me to the dormitory, I was bleeding almost everywhere on my body. They took me to the bathroom; they washed me. It was another torture taking a shower. Then we went to my closet and helped me change clothes and lay down on my bed. They stayed with me until diner time.

One of my friends went to see the housing director and asked for permission to bring me food in the dorm. He got it but the military on guard refused. The military told him:

"We have been instructed to guard all the students at the same place. They all have to be in the dining room together at the same time, they have to be in the information room together at the same time after the dinner, and then go together in to the dorm at the same *time. There is no exception. My friend asked the military: "Were you also ordered not to intervene when some students were beating and torturing their innocent classmates?" "That is not your business," the military replied. "You'd better bring him here, or I will do it myself." My friend complied and came to get me. He advised me to stay calm and courageous.*

Within fifteen minutes, I was in the dining room. Every eye was focused on me, as if they had never seen me. I was almost disfigured. One of my neighbours, sitting near me and looking at my wounds, just asked, "What happened to you Jean? I had nothing to tell him; because he knew since he passed by the basketball field when I was laid on the hot tiles, and I recognized him.

I could not eat; I just drank a cup of tea. I didn't even finish it, it was so disgusting. While some students I know were laughing at me, only P. Evariste encouraged me to eat. I remember he told me, "The night may be very long; you'd better put something in your stomach. Even though you throw it up, something will remain, and you will survive until tomorrow." I appreciated his advice, but whatever I touched seemed to be rotten and smelling already. I tried but I could not swallow anything.

It was day of collecting dishes, washing the tables, and going to the information room as we usually did in normal time. Looking around in the dining room, I could see many faces were absent, especially the Hutu. I knew already that the Hutu students from the superior cycle had almost all been arrested that morning. I began to wonder what I was still doing there, just waiting for my death according to what I endured in the afternoon. I stopped thinking about my life.

Meanwhile, N. Dismas from the 14th grade (last year of the superior cycle) threw a knife away towards my face; it missed by an inch my right ear and broke the window behind me. The noise generated by the knife in contact with the glass broke the unusual deep silence in the dining room. At the same time a bell rang. It was not usual. The lights were cut off in the dining room.
People began to run towards the nearest exit. I could hear some voices saying" We are attacked! We are attacked! We are attacked." I ran among others. Three minutes later, I was almost at the middle exit of the information and game room where I was grabbed by five classmates (S. Celestin, K. Salvator, M. Philippe, N. Gerard, M.Elie, and N. Thadee). It was as if they were waiting for me. I could see on the playgrounds many small Tutsi groups running in all directions with sticks in their hands. They were following Hutu students who tried to escape. Two minutes later all the lights went off all over the school campus. Gun shots were heard here and there. I was then immobilized on the ground; my five classmates began to beat me. S. Celestin planted a knife in my left arm, precisely in my wrist. It was very painful. I began to think about the death they had promised me in the afternoon. Cries of pain were heard all over the campus, the few Hutu students non- arrested and who survived the

afternoon ordeal were being beaten by Tutsi students. Anybody who dared to escape was shot.

The military did not intervene. I didn't have strength to cry. I knew it was useless, my fate was already sealed. I just concentrated my energy remembering the agony of the Christ. The last thought coming to my mind, was "God is my shepherd. I shall not want. He is in charge. He knows better than all my classmates what is good for me. I will not die because my fellows want it, I will certainly die in due time". The other thought that came through my mind and expressed by mouth was: "S. Celestin, K. Salvator, M. Philippe, N. Gerard, M. Elie, I forgive you". I then felt my last minute was coming and I silently asked God to forgive them.
While I was being beaten, more other cries could be heard all over the campus. My friend had warned me that in the evening the Tutsi had organized a generalized attack on all the remaining Hutu students. This would be interpreted as a self-defence against the Hutu. This would also justify the intervention of the military on the campus to arrest the remaining Hutu students. This information was very helpful to plan how to react to the beating since I could not flee from the campus. So, I didn't take it as a surprising accident, but as something prepared ahead. My mind was prepared to accept and endure and let go the Calvary. During the beating I was praying for my attackers, asking God to lessen my suffering and blessing my five classmates. I lost knowledge when a knife was

implanted in my left wrist. When my mind came back, the images of the Christ being crucified were mostly dominant. With the jet of blood, I cried," my Jesus, my God, have mercy on us." One lasting idea came to my mind, "Jesus was killed to save us. I was not saving anybody." It was so sad.

Beside me, and by his voice, I could recognize K. Lucien crying from the suffering. He was being beaten just five meters from where I was laying down. K. Artemon, another Hutu student, was being beaten a little far away. I heard them crying atrociously. I could recognize their voices. At that particular minute, N. Gerard released me and ran where K. Lucien was agonizing. Within seconds all my attackers left me and hurried to see K. Lucien and K. Artemon dying (Artemon was one of the strongest persons at our school). M. Elie, one of my last attackers lashed out: "We will come later to finish Jean; he is no longer a problem, he is very weak, as he does not move any more, and he is almost dead. Let us go and watch a Hutu like K. Lucien dying." K. Lucien was the best athlete at school, and second to me for the best grades in my class. He was also mostly outspoken against the Tutsi; for that he was the most hated Hutu in my class.

Instantly, I was just able to move my head to my right and my left. I saw K. Lucien and K. Artemon through the legs of their attackers lying in a flood of their blood. With all the energy I could get, I stood up and ran toward the North of the school compound. I will never be able to explain how I got enough energy to flee to the housing director, which was less than 100 meters from where I was beaten. It was a miracle to me. Within minutes I found myself inside that house. I could never explain how the military that guarded the director house let me get inside. From that house we could hear cries all over the campus. Sometimes we heard some gunshots. Maybe those who tried to cross the boundaries school were shot. But as the time went by lesser and lesser noise and gunshots were heard until the night became completely quiet.

I found myself inside that house with four other Tutsi (G. Prime, G. Alexander, Paul, and Sixte). They have also been beaten. I could not understand anything from that mystery since they were Tutsi. The director and his wife were outside the campus. That has always been another mystery for me how they could be absent when students needed them. We looked at each other strangely, but nobody talked to the other. We were ruminating the beating. We were all bleeding everywhere on our bodies. The only thing

Sixte said was, "Izo mbwa z'i Bururi tuzohonyora hamwe (Those dogs from Bururi will be crushed). I understood that they were taken for Hutu, and physically they strangely looked like Hutu.

From the director's house windows, we tried to look outside. There was a clear moon. We could see the military and Tutsi students amassing the dead bodies and packing them in the military trucks, taking them outside of the compound for unknown destination.

Two hours later the military guarding the director's house told us that the campus was now peaceful and clean from undesirable people. I realized they have taken me as a Tutsi. They asked us to join the other students on the school playground. The lights have been restored all over the campus. One of the militaries dared to tell us that the campus was clean, that no rebels were remaining at school. It was chilling in case they knew who I was. In their mind they could not imagine a Hutu running toward a Tutsi house. It was good for me it be so.

While they were escorting us to the dormitory, we just met the director and his wife coming in. They recognized me, showed compassion to me, and asked me to stay for a while with them. They knew my brother Yves very well; they had been good friends for a long time. But in my mind, I thought it was my end. The wife tried to comfort me, but she was astonished the way I was disfigured. She brought hot water and a towel to clean my wounds. She put some medicines on my wounds. They just called my brother's home to check if they could take me home to spend the night there. But nobody answered. "That is fine," he said. "You can go and spend the night with other students in the dormitory or stay here with us. Tomorrow I will take you home if you feel insecure here on the campus." My heart advised me to join other students in the dormitory.

Then the military took me in the dormitory. No question asked. They handed me over 3 military who were guarding my room. The rooms in the dormitory were big enough to house ten students. My room was almost empty, it contained two to three students. No question they were all Tutsi remaining in the dormitory. In my room two Tutsi were already in their beds, but they immediately woke up at the noise of the military boots. In fact, nobody was sleeping that night. Most of the students were hilarious for having defeated the enemies (Hutu students). They could not hide their joy and happiness. Most of them were counting their exploits: how many Hutu they have killed. How much money they stole from the Hutu killed, and many other details. The military in the dormitory were making sure that no rebels were still alive. They checked bed by bed. When they arrived at my bed, seeing my wounds, they were dubious and asked me,

"What happened to you". I answered that I was mistakenly beaten by my classmates." "You must be a rebel", one of them intoned. Before I even answered, another said, "Get up", while I was getting up, the military who saw me in the housing director said, "He was among the Tutsi who took refuge at the director house; I took time to observe him, I think he is one of us who was mistakenly taken as a Hutu. Even the director knows him if you consider the way he was compassionate and took care when he saw him."

The fourth one recognized that many other Tutsi were beaten unjustly. Then came the very difficult question: "Do you know someone else who can testify that you are not a rebel?" "Yes", I said. "Then give us a least three names" he continued. Instantly I gave the names of R. Lazare the housing director, N. Evariste, and K. Evariste, and N. Isidore from the 14th grade, K. Evariste was my classmate. I was afraid they would ask my roommates, but it did not matter for me. I answered their questions. "Give us ten minutes, we are going to check and we will be back to you", they told me. They left me.

Three of them went to check the next room. I began to sweat in case my roommates denounced me, but my mind quickly calmed my emotions and I heard as if an inner voice was telling me, "Don't worry God is in charge, you will survive to tell the story." After a while, I saw N. Evariste coming back with the military who was questioning me. Then he told the military:" I came personally to see the person they were questioning. My brother military," said N. Evariste ", don't doubt anymore on him, he is our brother.

Tomorrow we are going find out who did this to him. I know that many Tutsi students profited of the opportunity to express their anger to those they didn't like for many reasons. The student government association is going to investigate all the similar cases and ask the authorities to punish the abuses committed on innocent students. You can be sure, I know him very well. I take responsibility of any trouble he may cause." Then they left. He stayed and teased with me a little while before he went to sleep. He was completely shocked by the way I have been tortured. I could not sleep the whole night.

During the night, the military started explaining and showing us room by room how to manipulate the "kalashnikov" and bayonet. I did participate in the *training, but my heart was out of control. I asked God to be with me, to strengthen and not allow my fear or any other emotion to betray me and deliver me to the military. My heart was beating so hard that I began to sweat at the touch of the gun. But I was able to dominate my frustration and my fear. I stayed very calm. I did that to hide my internal heated emotion. I just didn't want to betray myself. After the training I went quietly in my bed wondering what the tomorrow would hold for me. I didn't try to sleep, it was quite impossible. My heart was beating so hard. I did not dare to go to the bathroom before I went in my bed. I was so terrified. I expected to die any time. When my roommates began to snore I just pretended I was sleeping, but I was watching all the movements of the students and the military.*

In the morning I took my bath like others. I clothed. I packed all my bloody clothes in the suitcase. All my precious things, money, and best shirts had been stolen. I put on the best clothes remaining and went for the breakfast with others. No other Hutu was on the campus. Many Tutsi would come and ask me how I survived; others would be kinder than they used to be, trying to comfort me in many ways. Two of them would tell me that they were going to find out the persons who beat me. Another told me that surviving in such condition proved I was really a man of God. I learned that the housing director had instructed the student association to assure my security and asked the students not to touch me.

I was terrified when the military brought in two other Hutu who had been beaten beyond recognition. They showed them during the breakfast and then took them in the dormitory to wash them. The military came back to ask the student government association to go and identify them. The SGA would tell us later that those students were dead before they could identify them. But they were all Hutu. The military put their bodies in their truck and took them away from the school.

I remember the student N. Dismas coming and telling me," Uracari ho? Turakwereka wa mbwa y'umuhutu we, ("Are you still alive? we are going to show you dog of Hutu"). I told him, "You cannot do anything against the will of God, you tried to blow my head with a table knife, but God is Great, He prevented it. I will not die because you want it. God is my protector. For you I am already dead, but you see I am still alive by the grace of Almighty God, our Lord.

I could not hold my breathe; I could not even take my breakfast. I looked in all directions to see if I could find any space to hide my face. They kept terrorizing and insulting me. A certain Lazare told me, "I cannot eat if there is still a Hutu among us".

He went to bring a military to arrest me. Two friends N. Evariste and K. Evariste went to talk to that military, and he didn't come to me. But I could not eat anything, I was full of nausea. My friends stayed with me until 10:00 am trying to comfort me.

At 10:30 am, all the students were instructed to clean the campus of the blood scattered almost everywhere, to collect the pieces of body. Some students had to carry water in buckets. I could see some students gathering pieces of body such fingers, legs, arms, toes, and heads of students killed the previous night by their classmates. Two to three buckets were filled of such pieces. It was atrocious thinking that human beings have been torn to pieces by their classmates. It was unbelievable but true. That was another hard time for me. This kept reminding me of my fellows who had been beaten till to death and cut into pieces by their classmates. At the same times, I was wondering why God kept me alive amidst this chaos. I felt guilty to have not prayed for them. The dead no longer suffer any more, this was my consolation. Since there were not enough hoses and tubes at our disposal, we had to look for water with jerry cans. My job was to oversee if all the corners of the campus got enough water to clean the mess. I was assigned to one fountain to supply water. I had to make sure everybody had enough water. Ten or fifteen bodies were found on the campus, but the military took care of them immediately. After we had cleaned all the mess, we were allowed to relax, wherever we wanted on the campus.

Others would offer to take me to hospital. It was too good to understand, and too strange to trust them, just unbelievable. I knew those excuses were empty words, but I had already forgiven them and asked God to forgive them too. At a special moment I met my best friends N.Evariste and K. Evariste while they were relaxing under a tree. They told me that I would not survive if I stay one more night on the campus. We even discussed a plan to leave the campus. N. Evariste would go and ask the permission from the military to enable us to meet or have more time together. For the lunch, I ate at the housing director. They didn't know the whereabouts of my brother. The director promised to stop by my brother's house once he went to town. I stayed in his house until 3 p.m. but the director did not come back to me. Instead he went to his office. The idea of going to check on my brother comforted me but at the same time I was confused that he did not answer the telephone the previous night. I guessed there was something wrong at home, but I could not know exactly what it was.

My flight from school and hiding

The kindness I had from some Tutsi known as just nasty people that day was unusual. Some would apologize that they had made a mistake. Two of my attackers the last night, N. Gerard and M. Elie, would present their excuses and asking for forgiveness. They all were ready to help me leave the campus. A group of six classmates along with the 2 Evariste took me in my classroom with a plan to leave the school. Three of them went to talk to the military outside, two others removed the glasses from the windows, the last one helped me to go over the class wall, go through the window and jump outside. Those who went to talk with the military outside the class accompanied me until I reach the nearest highway.

I went directly to my brother's house but he was no longer there. My sister in law told me she had not seen him since May 14, 1972. He was probably killed. She advised me not to stay there since there were military coming to search the house every evening. She was afraid to keep me there. She advised me to go to hide somewhere else. She gave me one hundred francs and begged me to leave. I went to see two other brothers in two other parts of the town. One of them was afraid to keep me. He had been arrested three times, and three times his Tutsi neighbors intervened. We went together to see if the third brother could provide me a safe place to stay. Once there they negotiated the landlord if she could hide me in her house. That landlord had already helped to pass the military barrages dressed on the road from Ngagara to Bwiza (they were 5). I stay in her house two months and half. By July 3, 1972, I had to go to the rural area because it was the summer break. I did not have problem traveling from the city to my home village.

The government has instructed the communal administrator to register any visitor who came from another commune. The Nyumba Kumi have to help the administration enforce the new rules. They came to my home the first day of my arrival and read me the injunction. The third day, I went to register and then was arrested by the administrator. The next day I was sent to the district commissioner (Commissaire d'arrondissement) where I stayed for 45 days in abject conditions. Then I was sent to Gitega prison where I stayed up to January 15, 1973.

At my release, I stayed with my parents up to April 28, 1973 when the communal administrator and military come to arrest me. Every Easter period there was a re-enactment of the 1972 events. I was able to escape and flee to Cibitoke Province. I unsuccessfully fled to Rwanda but I did not get a chance to be accepted as refugee. I was told that Burundi was peaceful and I was escorted to the Rwanda Burundi border after 10 days after I failed to get at least three Burundian refugees who could recognize me.

I was preparing to get married but another wave of arresting of Hutu in Cibitoke occurred. I fled to Zaire but I did stay to long because of the harsh conditions I was submitted to. I decide to go back and die in my country. By September 1973, God opened doors for me to go back to school and finish my high school. I was then able to attend the university and become a senior civil servant of my country.

TESTIMONY 6: AN INTERVIEW WITH A POLITICIAN FROM CNDD-FDD ON 29/12/2010 IN BUJUMBURA

I recall the genocide incidents since 1972; there was massacre of civilians in the southern parts of Burundi because of the Hutu extermination plan which was to be executed by Tutsis in April 1972. Michel Micombero regime came up with execution of an extermination plan of killing people especially from the Hutu ethnic group. They killed Hutu women, children and elderly people. In other parts like northern, eastern and western parts of Burundi where people were not aware of what was going on in the southern parts, Hutus found themselves being victims because influential Hutus such as students, businessmen, teachers, church leaders were being summoned by the government officials to go to prove their innocence. It is sad, they never came back! After 3 weeks almost 10 percent of the entire population was brutally killed and buried in mass graves. That was "a pure genocide" because the then government planned and executed this plan of killing civilians from Hutu ethnic group and 30 percent in 1972 fled the country".

TESTIMONY 7: AN INTERVIEW WITH A POLITICIAN FROM THE UPRONA ON 22/12/2010 IN BUJUMBURA

"Although I belong to the opposition party, I

have witnessed mass killings in Burundi equal to the genocide of Rwanda especially in 1960s, 1972, 1988 and 1993. This will not stop unless the current ruling party agrees to sit together with opposition parties in order to have a comprehensive political dialogue so that we can resolve our conflicts and bring the national unity and ultimately national healing"

TESTIMONY 8: AN INTERVIEW WITH A LAND COMMISSIONER IN RUMONGE ON 25/12/2010

"It is not easy to deal with land disputes especially the ones relating to refugees who fled the country in 1972. Sometimes when I am conciliating land disputes, I recall the genocide of 1972 when my father was killed"

TESTIMONY 9: AN INTERVIEW WITH A LOCAL ADMINISTRATOR ON MASS KILLINGS IN THE CHURCH IN MUGARA ON 26/12/2010

"My name (anonymous) I was born in Rumonge Mugara; although I am 47 years

old I still remember what happened in 1972. For example how we used to hide in the bushes and many Hutu people who were killed in the church, this was genocide because the targets by the Tutsi-led army were Hutus ..."

TESTIMONY 10: AN INTERVIEW WITH N. SYLIVESTRE ON 06/01/2011IN GITAZA

My name is N. Sylivestre, I was born in Muhuta, Mubanga in Bujumbura Rurale. I recall thousands and thousands of Hutus who were slaughtered under this mango tree in 1972 (refer to the picture in Annexure E). Meetings would be called upon by the then administrator by the name of Rudigi, blindly people would go to the meetings as they were told they needed to come to prove their innocence because the government was searching for "abamenje" or traitors. Upon arrival they would be queued. For example, a father would be asked to kill his own child or cut his private parts, fingers or toes and eat them. It is sad! My father Biranse and other Hutus were taken downhill by Tutsis from Mubanga to Gitaza market place, on their way the Tutsis would cut his flesh by using sharp knives and ask him to eat his own flesh, it is sad he died on his way to Gitaza in pain and agony. For few strong men who managed to reach their destiny would be spared and ordered to dig huge pits and gather dead bodies in the mass graves, lastly the spared would be forced to join their friends while still alive inside the pits and being shot to death. For local people this place is known as a "slaughtering place". I do not see why people advocate human rights, there are no human rights in Burundi, they are written only on the papers.[75]

TESTIMONY 11: AN INTERVIEW WITH SAHINGUVU

My name Is Sahinguvu, I am 60 years old. I was born in Mugara, the district of Rumonge in Bururi Province. I will not forget my loved ones including my father, mother and siblings who were killed in this church (See Annexure F) by Tutsi priests. As you can see, inside and outside of this church, corpses were scatted everywhere. I survived because, Tutsis thought I was dead and dead bodies fall over my back, I could not move. I managed to move only when the army went to bring trucks to remove the corpses inside the church. I was rolling like a snake a bit further and hid in the bush. Again down, there at the hot water spring a lot of slaughtering happened in 1972.

Names and ethnic groups of some officials assassinated in Burundi

Title or position held	Name and Surname	Ethnic Group	Year of Death
King	H.E Charles Ndizeye/ Ntare V	Tutsi	1972
President of Republic	-H.E Melchior Ndadaye	Hutu	1993
	-H.E Cyprien Ntaryamira	Hutu	1994
Speaker & Vice Speaker Of the Parliament	-Paul Mirerekano	Hutu	1965
	-Pontien Karibwami	Hutu	1993
	-Gilles Bimazubute	Tutsi	1993
	- NDIKUMWAMI Richard	Hutu	1993
	- NURWAKERA Joachim	Hutu	1993
	- MPFAYOKURERA Sylvestre	Hutu	1994
	- MANIRAMBONA	Hutu	1994

	Juvénal,		
	- NTAHOMVUKIYE Evariste	Hutu	1994
	- NDIKUMANA Innocent	Tutsi	1994
	- SURWAVUBA Malachie	Hutu	1995
	- GAHUNGU Gérard	Hutu	1996
	- NTAMUTUMBA Bibiane	Hutu	1996
	- MUBEMBE Emmanuel	Hutu	1996
	- Dr. SINDAYIHEBURA Innocent	Hutu	1996
	- Gabriel Gisabwamana	Hutu	1999
Prime Minister	-Louis Rwagasore	Tutsi	1961
	-Joseph Cimpaye	Hutu	1965
	-Paul Ngendandumwe	Hutu	1965
	-Joseph Bamina	Hutu	1965
Minister	-E. Nigane	Hutu	1965
	-Ignace Ndimanya	Hutu	1965
	-Andre Baremera	Hutu	1965

	-Emile Benyuje	Hutu	1965
	-Ferdinand Bitariho	Hutu	1965
	-Zacharie Ntiryica	Hutu	1965
	-Andre Ruramusura	Hutu	1965
	-Marc Ndayiziga	Hutu	1969
	-Barnabe Kanyaruguru	Hutu	1969
	-Cyprien Henehene	Hutu	1972
	-Pascal Bubiriza	Hutu	1972
	-JC Bandyambona	Hutu	1972
	- Martin Ndayahoze	Hutu	1972
	-Juvenal Ndayikeza	Hutu	1993
	-Benard Ciza	Hutu	1994
	- Dr Ig. Ernest Kabushemeye	Hutu	1995
	-Monsieur SIMBIZI Cyriaque	Tutsi	1994
	-Emmanuel Niyonkuru	Hutu	2017
Clergy	Bishop Gihimbare Gabriel	Hutu	1972
	Abbe Emile Ndigiriye	Hutu	1972
	Abbe Karenzo	Hutu	1972

	Théophile		
	Abbe Barampama André	Hutu	1972
	Abbe Samandari Thomas	Hutu	1972
	Abbe Ngeza Gabriel	Hutu	1972
	Abbe Ndarukerege Gervais	Hutu	1972
	Abbe Girukwigomba Sébastien	Hutu	1972
	Abbe Kayehe Pascal	Hutu	1972
	Abbe Simbandumwe Marcel	Hutu	1972
	Abbe Nsaguye Jerome	Hutu	1972
	Abbe Muteragiranwa F.xavier	Hutu	1972
	Abbe Gahungu Marc	Hutu	1972
	Abbe Hakizimana Astère	Hutu	1972
	Abbe Nzeyimana Donatien	Hutu	1972
	Abbe Nikoyagize Joseph	Hutu	1972

	Abbe Bivanda Melchior	Hutu	1972
	Abbe Gakwavu Martin	Hutu	1972
	Abbe Ntirampeba Paul	Hutu	1972
	-Abbe Ruhaya Protais	Hutu	1972
	-Abbe Kayoya Michel	Hutu	1972
	- Bishop Joachin Rukuna	Tutsi	1995
	-Abbe BIVUGIRE Anastase	Hutu	1972
	-Abbe SINANKWA Michel	Hutu	1972
	-Abbe BITARIHO Maximilien	Hutu	1972
	-Abbe HAVYARIMANA André	Hutu	1972
	-Abbe NDUWIMANA Zacharie	Hutu	1972
	- Abbe HAKIZIMANA Sylvestre	Hutu	1972
	- Abbe Cyrille NDABEMEYE	Hutu	1972

	- Abbe NTUKAMAZINA François	Hutu	1972
	- Abbe, Firmin NYEDETSE	Hutu	1972
	-Abbé Dieudonné NIYOYANDEMYE	Hutu	1972
	- Father Jacques NTAWITALIZO (Rwandese)	Hutu	1994
	- Abbe Guide RURANGIRWA	Hutu	1994
	- Father ALDO MALCHIOR	Hutu	1994
	-Father OTTORINO MAULE	Hutu	1994
	-Father CATINO GUBERT	Hutu	1995
Governors	- BIZIMANA Déo (Kirndo)	Hutu	1993
	- NZOBONIMPA Bède (Ngozi)	Hutu	1993
	- MVUTSE Sylvestre,(Cibitoke)	Hutu	1996

	- SENTAMO Englebert (Karuzi)	Tutsi	1995
	- SURWAVUBA Malachie (Kayanza)	Hutu	1995
	- NURWAKERA Joachim (Gitega)	Hutu	1995
	- NKURIKIYE Léonard (Advisor Kayanza)	Hutu	1995
	- NDIKUMANA Cassien (Advisor Rutana)	Hutu	1995
	- NTIBARUTAYE Fidèle (Advisor Ngozi)	Hutu	1995
	- NDAYISABA Athanase (Adv- Kayanza)	Hutu	1995
	- BIHWAYAGA Stanislas (Advisor Ruyigi)	Hutu	1995
	- NTIBWAMEZE Emmanuel (Ruyigi	Hutu	1995
	- RUSINE Augustin (Advisor Bururi)	Hutu	1996

Many people were lucky enough to escape from attempts while others were wounded. Pastors, ministers, catholic priests, sisters and brothers were killed as well as many staff member of different departments of public services and university students even high school students. Principals and professors were assassinated publicly by their students without mercy under supervision of Tutsi army and police because they were only from Hutu ethnic group. The population powerlessly watched the bloodshed made by the army, the police and Tutsi militias. Those memories are requiring in minds of many. Many attempts to falsify facts and the entire history took place.

Filtered through the prism of ethnicity, collective memories only bear a distant relationship to the facts. The experience of traumatic events creates its own universe of discourse, where the "other" is seen as belonging to a sub-human category. This is also true of individual memories, and it applies to both Tutsi and Hutu. But given that the loss of Hutu lives was vastly superior to the Tutsi's, it is easy to see why Hutu memories have been particularly prone to Manichean representations.

The phenomenon is nowhere more vividly captured than in Liisa Malkki's discussion of "the mythico-history of atrocity", based on open-ended interviews with Hutu refugees in Tanzania (Malkki, 1995: 91 ff). She shows how memories of atrocity mutate into a sickening, ghoulish depiction of the tortures inflicted by Tutsi: "There was a manner of cutting the stomach (of a pregnant woman). Everything that was found in the interior was lifted out... The cadaver of the mama, the cadaver of the baby of the future, they rotted on the road. Not even a burial. The mother was obliged to eat the finger of her baby... The

Tutsi girls were given bamboos. They were made to kill by pushing the bamboo from below [from the vagina] to the mouth" (Ibid. 91). The aim here is the demonization of all Tutsi; in the minds of her interviewees the thread of evil goes way back, from the history of Tutsi penetration into the country to the present time: "The dehumanization of the Tutsi at this level acted as a culmination of earlier assertions in the mythico-history that the Tutsi did not belong to the 'nation' in its pure, 'natural' state" (Ibid, 93). Stripped of their hype, Malkki's interviews capture a recurrent theme in the discourse of Hutu extremists: the innate perversity of the Tutsi "race". While the past is instrumentalized to demonstrate the evil dispositions of the Tutsi "race", the present is re-interpreted in a way that confirms the fundamental goodness of the Hutu: there is no reference to the challenge posed by the Hutu insurrection, let alone to the acts of courage displayed by Tutsi to protect their Hutu neighbors. Much of this, along with a lengthy reconstruction of Burundi's pre-colonial past as a story of good guys vs. bad guys, is articulated in what later became the manifesto of Hutu extremists, an undated document by the late Rémi Gahutu titled "Persecution of the Hutu of Burundi" (Gahutu, n.d.). Insofar as they grossly amplify an all too tragic reality, Hutu memories bring into sharp focus the traumatic psychological impact of the experience of mass violence.

For some Hutu analysts the so-called rebellion is yet another irrefutable proof of Tutsi perfidy. Not only did the government fail to take any action to nip the insurrection in the bud – despite its awareness that it was being planned – but in fact did everything it could to facilitate the explosion, the better to justify the ensuing genocidal bloodbath. What happened in last days of April was the tragic outcome of a government-inspired manipulation, aimed at justifying the next step – the mass eradication of Hutu populations. Such, in brief, is the argument set forth by the historian Augustin Nsanze (Nsanze, 2003, 214-218), which to this day forms a key leitmotiv in the imaginings of Hutu extremists.

Where Hutu memories frequently elude references to the called Hutu insurrection, Tutsi memories, on the other hand, give pride of place to the mortal threat posed to their community by Hutu rebels. Genocidal intent is the key presumption. As if to strengthen the force of the argument, the number of Tutsi casualties is deliberately inflated, and so, also, the number of rebels, with the figure of 25,000 sometimes cited as fact (Shibura, 1973: 96). To mobilize so many people requires "a lot of time and colossal resources", writes [Albert Shibura->282], a key participant in the repression (Ibid.) The unstated assumption is that a large number of people killed is irrefutable proof of genocide. Another is that it has happened before. Thus the massacre of hundreds of Tutsi (here again there are no reliable estimates) by the authors of the abortive 1965 coup are described by Shibura as "the genocide of October 19, 1965", abetted by outside actors, including the CIA (Ibid. 58). Allegations of a Hutu-inspired plot in 1969 are again portrayed as involving "an attempted genocide" of Tutsi what is totally wrong (Ibid. 76). Every instance of Hutu violence is thus cited as proof of a genocidal thread running from 1965 to 1972. Furthermore, despite "the barbaric conspiracy of some 25,000 nationals and foreigners", to quote from the Burundi ambassador to Brussels, Laurent Nzeyimana, "there is no ethnic or tribal problem in Burundi". His argument is straightforward: if the externally abetted plot has in no way diminished the cohesion of Hutu and Tutsi, this is because inter-ethnic harmony is inherent in Burundi society, and because the majority of the people know that the prophylactic measures taken by the government were only directed at those elements involved in the conspiracy.

With the passage of time, many of these outrageous claims are receding from public and private memories. Furthermore, beginning with the Arusha conference and the opening of the political arena to opposition groups, a genuine transformation has taken place in the country's political climate. Most importantly, ethnicity has ceased to operate as the central axis of Burundi politics. All of which, along with the promise of a Truth and Reconciliation Commission, raises hopes that accusations based on invective and twisted evidence may in time yield to a more dispassionate exchange. Taking into consideration those men and women killed since 1965, what had been said and written was totally wrong. Hutu were victim of conspiracy, lies and their blood were shed without mercy.

CHAP.V The intervention of the international community

Since Burundi's independence in 1962, there have been two events called genocides in the country but along years there had been people disappearing, killed and buried in Musgraves. The 1972 mass killings of Hutus by the Tutsi-dominated army, and the 1993 mass killings are both described as genocides in the final report of the International Commission of Inquiry for Burundi presented to the United Nations Security Council in 1996 but none has been recognized.

A.   The effort of the UN on the matter of Burundi since 2005

November 2017: On 20 the Special Envoy of the Secretary-General for Burundi Michel Kafando and the chair of the Peacebuilding Commission Burundi Configuration, Ambassador Jürg Lauber (Switzerland), briefed the Council on the situation in Burundi (S/PV.8109). The briefing was followed by consultations.

August 2017: On 2, the Council adopted a presidential statement, expressing concern over the political situation and ongoing violence in Burundi and strongly urging the government and all parties to immediately cease and reject such violence. The Council further reiterated its full support to the Secretary-General and his Special Envoy in their efforts to engage the government of Burundi on the modalities of the implementation of resolution 2303.

July 2017: On 26, the Council received a briefing, followed by consultations, on the situation in Burundi from Special Envoy Michel Kafando and Ambassador Jürg Lauber of Switzerland, the chair of the Peacebuilding Commission's Burundi configuration.

June 2017: On 20, the Council was briefed on the situation in Burundi by Assistant Secretary-General for Political Affairs, Tayé-Brook Zerihoun. The Permanent Representative of Switzerland, Jürg Lauber, also briefed in his capacity as chair of the Peacebuilding Commission's Burundi configuration. During his briefing, Zerihoun reported that the situation in Burundi remained volatile, human rights abuses continued to be reported, and there was increased incitement of hatred and violence by and within the Imbonerakure.

March 2017: On 9, the Council was briefed by Jamal Benomar, Special Adviser to the Secretary-General, on his latest report on the situation in Burundi. Benjamin William Mkapa, East African Community facilitator of the Inter-Burundian Dialogue, and Ambassador Jürg Lauber (Switzerland), Chair of the Burundi configuration of the Peacebuilding Commission, also briefed the Council. The briefing was followed by consultations. On 13 March, Council members issued a press statement expressing their concern about the humanitarian and human rights situation in the country and the slow progress in the Inter-Burundian dialogue.

November 2016: On 8, the Secretary-General's Special

Adviser, Jamal Benomar, briefed Council members in consultations on his recent meetings in the region and on the Secretary-General's report on the situation in Burundi.

October 2016: The Secretary-General's Special Adviser, Jamal Benomar, briefed Council members in consultations on 13 October before departing for the region. Council members issued a press statement the following day, calling on Burundi to cooperate with Benomar "to develop, in a consensual manner, a plan and timeline" for the implementation of resolution 2303 of 29 July.

July 2016: On 29, the Council adopted resolution 2303, establishing a UN police component in Burundi of 228 police officers for an initial period of one year to monitor the security and human rights situation in the country. The resolution also requested the Secretary-General to take the necessary steps for the protection of the deployed UN personnel and facilities in consultation with Burundi and urged Burundi, to cooperate with the deployment and activities of the police component.

April 2016: On 1, the Council adopted resolution 2279 requesting the Secretary-General to provide options for a police component to increase UN presence in Burundi (S/PV.7664). The options were submitted on 15 April and discussed by Council members under "any other business" on 27 April.

March 2016: On 18, Secretary-General Ban Ki-moon, UN High Commissioner for Human Rights Zeid Ra'ad Al Hussein and Ambassador Jürg Lauber (Switzerland), chair of the Burundi configuration of the Peacebuilding Commission, briefed the Council on the situation in Burundi. The Burundian Minister for External Relations and International Cooperation, Alain Nyamitwe, and Ambassador Tuvako Manongi (Tanzania) also addressed the Council.

February 2016: On 10, Council members were briefed by Special Adviser Jamal Benomar in consultations on the situation in Burundi. In late February, Council members negotiated a draft presidential statement that expressed the Council's intention to strengthen the UN's presence in Burundi.

December 2015: On 11, Council members were briefed in consultations under "any other business" by Special Adviser Jamal Benomar on the situation in Burundi. Council members also discussed Burundi under "any other business" on 14 December. On 19 December, Council members issued a press statement, noting the AU decision to deploy an African prevention and protection mission in Burundi, and called on all Burundian stakeholders to fully comply with it. The statement also highlighted the importance of UN contingency planning to develop options for the international community to respond to any further deterioration in the country.

November 2015: On 9, the Council was briefed by Under-Secretary-General for Political Affairs Jeffrey Feltman; High Commissioner for Human Rights Zeid Ra'ad Al Hussein (via video teleconference from Geneva); Ambassador Jurg Lauber, the Permanent Representative of Switzerland to the UN and chair of the PBC's Burundi Configuration (via video teleconference from Bujumbura); the Special

Adviser for the Prevention of Genocide Adama Dieng (via video teleconference from Jordan); and AU Ambassador to the UN Téte Antonio (S/PV.7553). On 12 November, the Council adopted resolution 2248, expressing its intention to consider additional measures against all Burundian who contribute to the perpetuation of violence. The resolution also requested the Secretary-General to update the Council within 15 days, including by presenting options on the future presence of the UN in the country. At press time, it seemed that update might be scheduled for 30 November.

October 2015: On 21, at the request of France, Council members were briefed in consultations on the situation in Burundi, by Under-Secretary-General for Political Affairs Jeffrey Feltman. On 28 October, the Council adopted a presidential statement taking note of the recent 17 October AU communique on Burundi (PSC/PR/COMM.(DLI)), expressing its concern about the growing insecurity in Burundi and continuing violence, condemning human rights abuses and calling for dialogue between all stakeholders.

August 2015: On 4, Council members issued a press statement condemning the killing of General Adolphe Nshimirimana in Bujumbura on 2 August and the violent attack on human rights activist Pierre Claver Mbonimpa on 3 August (SC/11996). Council members also expressed concern over the rapidly deteriorating security situation in Burundi and called on all political actors to resume an inclusive dialogue without delay. On 10 August, Council members were briefed in consultations on the situation in Burundi by Assistant Secretary-General for Political Affairs Tayè-Brook Zerihoun and Assistant Secretary-General for Human Rights Ivan Šimonović. On 28 August, at the request of France, the Assistant Secretary-General for Political Affairs Tayé-Brook Zerihoun briefed Council members on the political and security situation in Burundi under "any other business", an update was also provided on the process to appoint a UN mediator.

July 2015: On 2, Council members were briefed in consultations under "any other business", at the request of France, on the situation in Burundi following the controversial parliamentary and municipal elections. On 9 July, Assistant Secretary-General for Political Affairs Tayé-Brook Zerihoun and High Commissioner for Human Rights Zeid Ra'ad Al Hussein briefed the Council, followed by consultations. Following the presidential elections of 21 July, Council members were briefed by Zerihoun and the Deputy Head of the UN Electoral Observation Mission in Burundi (MENUB), Issaka Souna, in consultations on 28 July. A report by MENUB had previously been circulated to the Council earlier in the month.

June 2015: Council members were briefed on Burundi on 4 June by the Secretary-General's Special Envoy for the Great Lakes, Said Djinnit, and by Adama Dieng, the Secretary-General's Special Adviser for the Prevention of Genocide. Djinnit updated Council members on the East African Community emergency summit on Burundi on 31 May in Dar es Salaam. Dieng briefed on his recent visit to the country and warned that violence may escalate into an ethnic conflict. On 26 June, the Council adopted a presidential statement calling on the political parties in Burundi to participate in an inclusive dialogue in the "spirit of the Arusha Agreements and the Constitution" on what is needed to create conducive conditions for the elections.

May 2015: On 8, Special Envoy for the Great Lakes Said Djinnit briefed Council members in consultations via video teleconference on his mediation efforts between the government and the opposition in Burundi. In elements to the press, Council members expressed concern over the influx of refugees into neighboring states and called on all sides to refrain from violence. On 14 May, Djinnit briefed Council members in consultations again after an attempted coup against Burundian President Pierre Nkurunziza. Council members agreed on press elements that condemned attempts to seize power unlawfully and called for the swift return of the rule of law and the holding of credible elections in the spirit of the Arusha Agreements. The next day, Council members issued a press statement calling for the establishment of a genuine dialogue between all Burundians to create the necessary conditions for credible elections (SC/11896). On 24 May, Council members issued another press statement condemning the killing of opposition leader Zedi Feruzi on 23 May in Bujumbura (SC/11905). On 27 May, Djinnit briefed Council members again in consultations via video teleconference on his latest mediation efforts.

April 2015: On 16, Council members were briefed in consultations by Assistant Secretary-General for Political Affairs Tayé-Brook Zerihoun on recent developments in Burundi. On 17 April, Council members issued a press statement, stressing that the government and political opposition should refrain from any acts of violence and intimidation before, during and after the upcoming elections (SC/11864). Council members further noted their intention to follow closely and to respond to any actions in Burundi that threaten the peace, security or stability of Burundi. On 29 April, Special Envoy for the Great Lakes Said Djinnit was expected to brief Council members under "any other business" via video teleconference from Bujumbura on the situation.

March 2015: Council members visited the Central African Republic (CAR), Burundi and the AU headquarters in Addis Ababa from 10 to 13 March (S/2015/162). Angola and France co-led the visit to CAR and Addis Ababa. The CAR visit assessed progress and challenges facing MINUSCA and gave Council members an opportunity to meet with the transitional authorities on the political process, including preparations for elections. In addition to their activities in Bangui, Council members went to Bria in eastern CAR to visit local authorities, civil society and ex-Séléka members. On 12 March, the Council held its Ninth Annual Joint Consultative Session Meeting with the AU Peace and Security Council. Following an additional week of negotiations, a communiqué on the joint session was issued (S/2015/212). Angola, France and the US co-led the Burundi visit where Council members met with MENUB, the UN Country Team, government officials, other political actors and civil society. The focus of these discussions was whether President Pierre Nkurunziza would seek a third term, which the opposition contests would violate the constitution and could lead to violence. In the meeting with Nkurunziza, Council members stressed that he take actions that ensure the country's unity. France and Angola briefed the Council on the visiting mission on 18 March (S/PV.7407).

February 2015: On 18, the Council adopted a presidential statement marking the termination of the mandate of BNUB on 31 December 2014. The Council welcomed the significant progress achieved in Burundi while noting that several challenges remain to ensure that progress is not reversed, including reports of intimidation, harassment, political violence, arbitrary arrest and detention and other curtailments of the rights of freedom of peaceful assembly and expression of political actors. The Council also stressed the crucial need for a free, transparent, credible, inclusive and peaceful electoral process in 2015.

January 2015: On 21, the Council was briefed by Under-Secretary-General for Political Affairs Jeffrey Feltman on the final report of the Secretary-General on the UN Office in Burundi (S/2015/36), the mission's mandate ended on 31 December 2014 (S/PV.7364). The chair of the Burundi configuration of the Peacebuilding Commission Paul Seger (Switzerland) also briefed the Council. The meeting was followed by consultations.

November 2014: On 5, the Council was briefed by Parfait Onanga-Anyanga, the head BNUB, and Paul Seger (Switzerland) who chairs the PBC Burundi configuration (S/PV.7295). Zacharie Gahutu of Burundi's Ministry of Foreign Affairs and International Cooperation also addressed the Council. The briefing was followed by consultations after which the president of the Council, Gary Quinlan (Australia), released elements to the press. He said that Council members are monitoring the situation in Burundi and are looking forward to the establishment of the electoral observer mission after BNUB's drawdown on 31 December. He added that Council members encourage the government to create conditions for an inclusive electoral process and support the understanding reached with the government on the continued presence of the Office of the High Commissioner for Human Rights in Burundi after BNUB's drawdown.

August 2014: On 6, the Council was briefed by the Special Representative and head of BNUB, Parfait Onanga-Anyanga on the latest BNUB report. Onanga-Anyanga expressed his continuing concern about deep political divisions in the country, the lack of political dialogue on major national issues and restrictive laws on freedom of expression. He added that preparations were underway to withdraw BNUB by 31 December.

July 2014: Assistant Secretary-General for Human Rights Ivan Šimonović briefed Council members in consultations on 10 July on his 25-27 June visit to Burundi. Special Representative and head of BNUB, Parfait Onanga-

Anyanga, also briefed via video-teleconference. Addressing the Council, Šimonović expressed concern about politically motivated violent attacks by the Imbonerakure on political adversaries and the deep divide between political parties and that certain pieces of legislation could potentially shift political divisions back towards ethnic conflict if they were not implemented in an unbiased and fair manner. Onanga-Anyanga spoke about the need to maintain a monitoring role for the Office of the High Commissioner on Human Rights in Burundi following BNUB's departure.

May 2014: On 14, the Council was briefed via video-teleconference by the Special Representative and head of BNUB, Parfait Onanga-Anyanga, and by the chair of the Burundi configuration of the Peacebuilding Commission, Ambassador Paul Seger (Switzerland). The Minister for Interior of Burundi, Edouard Nduwimana, also addressed the Council. Council members held consultations with Onanga-Anyanga following the briefing.

April 2014: Council members were briefed on the situation in Burundi on 8 April by the head of the Department of Political Affairs, Under-Secretary-General Jeffrey Feltman, who informed the Council about the recent reports of increased violent activities by the Imbonerakure, the youth wing of the CNDD-FDD. Council members issued a press statement on 10 April, expressing concern over acts of intimidation, harassment and violence committed by youth groups in Burundi and calling for the government to hold the perpetrators accountable (SC/11350). The Council was briefed again in consultations on Burundi by Feltman, at the request of the US, on 24 April for an update on the situation on the ground.

March 2014: On 26, at the initiative of the US, Council members were briefed in consultations by Assistant Secretary-General for Political Affairs Tayé-Brook Zerihoun on the situation in Burundi.

February 2014: On 13, the Council adopted resolution 2137, extending the mandate of BNUB until 31 December 2014 (S/PV.7110). The Council also requested the Secretary-General to prepare BNUB's transition and transfer of responsibilities to the UN country team by that date.

January 2014:The Secretary-General's Special Representative and head of BNUB, Parfait Onanga-Anyanga, and the chair of the Burundi configuration of the Peacebuilding Commission (PBC), Ambassador Paul Seger (Switzerland), briefed the Council on BNUB on 28 January (S/PV.7104). Onanga-Anyanga told the Council that the recommendation to extend the political presence in Burundi was based on the evaluation of peacebuilding benchmarks and took into account the fact that a country team would not be able to absorb the mission's tasks at that time. Burundi's foreign minister also addressed the Council, stating that the UN country team could provide support for the June 2015 elections and so there was no justification to extend BNUB's mandate.

July 2013: On 22, Special Representative of the Secretary-

General and head of BNUB, Parfait Onanga-Anyanga, and the head of the Peacebuilding Commission's Burundi configuration, Ambassador Paul Seger (Switzerland), briefed the Council. Ambassador Herménégilde Niyonzima (Burundi) also participated. The briefings were followed by consultations.

February 2013: On 13, the Council adopted resolution 2090, extending the mandate of BNUB until 15 February 2014 (S/PV.6918). The Council requested the Secretary-General to provide a briefing by the end of July 2013 and a report by 17 January 2014 on the implementation of BNUB's mandate.

January 2013: On 24, Special Representative and head of BNUB Parfait Onanga-Anyanga briefed the Council on developments and the Secretary-General's latest report on BNUB. In his briefing, Onanga-Anyanga warned of the undermining effect that the distrust between the government and the opposition could have on holding successful elections scheduled for 2015. Chair of the PBC-Burundi configuration, Ambassador Paul Seger (Switzerland), also briefed the Council, noting the importance of BNUB's presence in Burundi until 2015. Albert Nshingiro, Permanent Secretary at the Ministry of Foreign Affairs and International Cooperation of Burundi told the Council that BNUB should be converted into a UN country team in 12 months. The briefing was followed by consultations.

July 2012: On 5, the Council heard a briefing by the Secretary-General's Special Representative and outgoing head of BNUB. The Chairperson of the Burundi PBC configuration also briefed. The briefing was followed by consultations attended by the Special Representative and Council members. On 26 July, the Council sent a letter to the Secretary-General, requesting data and assessments for each issue mentioned in the benchmarks, including observations on timing, trends and the role of BNUB in their implementation.

June 2012: On 7, the Secretary-General appointed Parfait Onanga-Anyanga (Gabon) as the new Special Representative and head of BNUB.

May 2012: On 10, the Secretary-General sent a letter to the Council with benchmarks and indicators for the future evolution of BNUB in the fields of security and stability, democratic process, transitional justice, governance and institution-building, rule of law, human rights, regional integration and social and economic development.

December 2011: On 20, the Council adopted resolution 2027, extending BNUB's mandate until 15 February 2013 under the same terms as the previous mandate, stressing that BNUB should support Burundi's efforts in the area of socioeconomic development. It requested that the Secretary-General update the Council by 31 May on the development of benchmarks for the evolution of BNUB into a UN country team presence and that a briefing be held in July. This followed a briefing by the Special Representative of the Secretary-General on 7 December, on the most recent Secretary-General's report, which recommended that BNUB's mandate be renewed at its current composition.

May 2011: The Special Representative of the Secretary-General and Head of BNUB briefed the Council.

February 2011: On 2, the Council held an "informal interactive dialogue" with the Chair of the Burundi configuration of the PBC and the Special Representative of the Secretary-General.

December 2010: The Secretary-General named Karin Landgren of Sweden as his special representative and head of the UN Office in Burundi (BNUB) on 31 December. On 16 December, the Council adopted resolution 1959 to reconfigure BINUB into the new UN Office in Burundi (BNUB) with effect 1 Jan 2011. BNUB will have a scaled-down structure and mandate aimed to support democracy- and institution-building efforts and establish the foundations for sustainable development. On 9 December the outgoing head of BINUB briefed the Council on the Secretary-General's latest report.

June 2010: On 23, the Council issued a press statement that called on all political stakeholders to participate fully in the elections and to respect the results of presidential elections to be held on 28 June. In those polls, President Pierre Nkurunziza was re-elected unopposed after opposition candidates boycotted the presidential elections because of allegations of fraud in local elections; EU observers have reportedly said that the elections met international norms.

May 2010: The Security Council was briefed on upcoming elections by BINUB's head and representatives of Burundi and Switzerland (who chairs the PBC country-specific configuration for Burundi) on 10 May.

March 2010: The Secretary-General appointed Charles Petrie as the head of BINUB on 25 March.

January 2010: On 15, following unsuccessful attempts by the Secretary-General to convince the government to reconsider its request that the Secretary-General recall his Special Representative, the Secretariat briefed Council members in consultations.

December 2009: At the end of December, the government of Burundi requested that Youssef Mahmoud be recalled from his position as Executive Representative of the Secretary-General to Burundi and head of BINUB. On 17 December the Council adopted a resolution extending the mandate of BINUB until 31 December 2010. On 10 December the then-head of BINUB briefed the Council on the Secretary-General's report on the country.

23 November 2009: Ambassador Maurer briefed the Configuration on his visit to Burundi and reported on the need to explore the idea of a long-term observation of the electoral process.

10 to 11 November 2009: Ambassador Peter Maurer, chair of the Burundi Configuration, visited Burundi to review the progress of peacebuilding and follow up on issues raised during the configuration's October meeting.

3 September 2009: The Secretary-General wrote to the Council on the findings of the electoral needs assessment mission sent to Burundi.

29 July 2009: The Burundi Configuration completed its third

semi-annual review of the implementation of the Strategic Framework for Peacebuilding in Burundi.

29 June 2009: The Permanent Representative of Switzerland, Ambassador Peter Maurer, took over as chair of the Burundi Configuration.

9 June 2009: The Council was briefed by Executive Representative of the Secretary-General and head of BINUB, Youssef Mahmoud.

25 to 27 May 2009: The then-chair of the PBC, Anders Liden, visited Burundi to assess progress in peacebuilding and identify key priorities for further engagement by including the elections in 2010.

6 February 2009: The PBC Burundi configuration held its second biannual review of the implementation of the Strategic Framework for Peacebuilding in Burundi and adopted recommendations (PBC/3/BDI/3)

11 December 2008: The Council was briefed by Charles Nqakula, Facilitator of the Burundi Peace Process and Minister of Defense of South Africa. He told the Council that the Comprehensive Ceasefire Agreement should be fully in place by 31 December.

17 July 2008: The PBC Organizational Committee elected Sweden to succeed Norway as chair of the Burundi country-specific configuration.

23 June 2008: The first biannual review of the progress and challenges to the Burundi Strategic Framework was held by the PBC, and recommendations of the review adopted (PBC/2/BDI/9).

27 May 2008: The Burundi configuration of the PBC

convened a thematic meeting on finding sustainable solutions to land issues, in light of the return of refugees from Tanzania to the country and the anticipated implications in terms of the need for additional resources to mitigate associated challenges.

10-15 May 2008: A delegation of seven members of the PBC's Burundi configuration travelled to Burundi on a field mission to obtain first-hand information about the situation on the ground, especially on renewed hostilities between the Palipehutu-FNL and the National Defense Forces of Burundi, following attacks by the Palipehutu-FNL in April 2008 and the stalemate in parliament.

24 April 2008: The Council issued a statement expressing concern about the security situation in Burundi and its intention to consider "possible additional measures in support of peace and stability" in the country.

27 and 28 February 2008: Ambassador Johan Løvald of Norway, chair of the PBC's country-specific configuration for Burundi, visited Washington, D.C. to discuss the priorities of Burundi with the Bretton Woods institutions and the US government.

February 2008: Forty-six Burundian opposition members wrote to the UN Secretary-General requesting protection after receiving death threats and alleging a "death list" of 350 opposition members.

27 November 2007: The PBC finalized its Monitoring and Tracking Mechanism (PBC/2/BDI/4) for the Strategic Framework for Peacebuilding in Burundi.

5-7 September 2007: Chairman of the Peacebuilding

Commission's country specific configuration on Burundi visited the country to follow-up on the situation on the ground.

13 August 2007: An informal consultation of the Burundi configuration of the PBC was convened to discuss the deteriorating political situation.

20 June 2007: The PBC endorsed the Strategic Framework for Peacebuilding in Burundi.

May 2007: During a May visit by the UN High Commissioner for Human Rights, Louise Arbour, the Burundian government agreed to the creation of a truth and reconciliation commission along with a tribunal to try people who committed atrocities during the civil war.

11-14 April 2007: A PBC delegation visited Burundi.

14-15 March 2007: A Burundi donors' roundtable was held in Bujumbura.

1 January 2007: BINUB commenced work.

November 2006: The Secretary-General in November released a report on Children and Armed Conflict in Burundi, which identified possible violators.

6 November 2006: The withdrawal of ONUB contingents was adjusted to allow them to assist with tasks of the Ceasefire Agreement with the "Forces Nationales de Liberation" (FNL), before the AU Special Task Force is put in place.

25 October 2006: The Council adopted resolution 1719 setting up UN Integrated Office in Burundi (BINUB) and establishing its mandate.

13 October 2006: The Peacebuilding Commission

discussed Burundi and recommended it for assistance from the Peacebuilding Fund which was launched on 11 October.

June 2006: A Secretary-General's report recommended the establishment of the UN Integrated Office in Burundi (BINUB), in order to consolidate and reinforce the humanitarian and development activities of ONUB.

December 2005: The withdrawal of 40 percent of the UN troops began, following the Council's decision to renew ONUB until 1 July 2006 in resolution 1650.

23 August 2005: Secretary-General Kofi Annan proposed a peacebuilding commission for Burundi to settle problems after the eventual withdrawal of ONUB.

After the 2015 crisis, different commissions visited the country several times including the Security Council and the UN Secretary General himself.

The international community does not feel the need of digging deep into the root of the evil of the Burundian nation while the cure can be found for the bitterness.

Conclusion

It would be a disservice to end this petition-advocacy without stressing that the need for healing of the nation of Burundi goes along with the need for Rwanda's healing. Rwanda has lost millions among its children, Hutu and Tutsi. The country has millions of refugees and many other wandering and stateless young people. As we saw in the description of the Burundi's still unrecognized genocide, Tutsi Rwandese have played a major role in the traumatic and tragic events of Burundi. Rwandan, Paul Kagame, falsely accuses Burundi of sheltering "Interahamwe" while the he recruited Burundian refugees, including children, at a refugee camp in eastern Rwanda and trained them for two months to unseat President Nkurunziza. Despite having much in common, Burundi and Rwanda have not had the best of relationships since 1965. The political crisis in Burundi over President Pierre Nkurunziza's third term, has further strained relationship between both countries. Burundi and Rwanda share similar cultures, ethnic divides and economic challenges. They share a colonial heritage of being governed as one territory by the Belgian colonialists. Both have experienced complicated violent conflicts related to ethnic divisions and have remained fragile nations. The healing of the Burundi nation must coincide with the healing of Rwandese.

Tensions between both countries today are paroxysmal and an open military war can erupt at any time between both nations. We know there are many western countries supporting Rwanda to attack Burundi, but there are also local and eastern countries that will support Burundi. The fact is that Rwanda is trying to recover from a recognize genocide and Burundi is struggling to recover from a long-time unrecognized genocide. Therefore, the positive role of the international community would be to prevent protagonists from inducing the crumpled and broken hearts of the two nations. The war between both countries will not only attempt to eradicate the two nations but also will not spare Democratic Republic Congolese, Ugandans and Tanzanians.

The plight of the Hutu people of the Great Lakes of Africa is similar to that of pigeons in major Western metropolitan areas with "Do not feed the pigeons" sign in public parks. The meaning is seemingly self-explanatory? First one must ask what disqualifies a pigeon from needing food, as other birds, to survive. Followed by seeing that what the sign is really trying to say is that there are too many pigeons, and anything that kills them or otherwise makes their lives difficult, such as lack of food is more than welcome. Instead the sign should read" Kill the pigeons", but, that would be uncivilized. Similarly, the Hutu people are the only people in the world to whom the International Community seems to have come to a tacit understanding that the conventional rules of **democracy, justice and self-determination** should not apply- "Do not feed the pigeons". This is the only explanation for crimes that are committed against the Hutus not to be investigated or even when investigated, the findings are shelved, never be talked about again.

With the respect I have for all ethnic groups in the nation of Rwanda, I submit that the country needs healing just as Burundi needs healing. From the history, according to many studies of being enslavement by Tutsi overlords for more than 400 years, to the genocide in Burundi, genocide in Congo and in Rwanda that stirs such controversy at the simple mention of genocides and brings trouble to anyone who dares to talk about these problems. Canadian Journalist, Judi River, most definitely experience problems caused from peaking about these genocides. After having dared to write about the crimes committed by the Tutsi led RPF Government, she subsequently had her life threatened in her own country, Canada, by Kagame's death squads. The simple fact of acknowledging the existence of Hutu people is considered a crime in Rwanda. Acknowledging, Hutu existence is seen as having a genocide ideology and it is punishable by law. Yet there are myriad of books and websites about courageous Tutsi people. Hutus suffered centuries of incredible oppression by a Tutsi monarchy whose supremacist ideology could have rivalled or surpassed by far, that of Apartheid in South Africa and Nazi Germany, but it seems not to have occurred. Since the 1960's the Tutsi Elite has managed to flip the script and has successfully made Hutus look and sound like blood thirsty monsters that are out to kill the innocent helpless

Tutsis for no reason. With the assistance of modern communications and public relations tools at their disposal, this narrative has taken hold to the point where these Tutsi lobbies claim, with total disregard, that the 1959 popular revolution that ended the monarchy in Rwanda was a genocide and that a Hutu president planned the genocide and used himself to be the first victim by having his own wife shoot his plane out of the skies.

This intense and well-crafted media campaign against the Hutus "Interahamwe or Imbonerakure" explains why no one has really tried to determine what happened to the millions of Hutus who died between 1965 and 1996 in the hands of Tutsi minority (UPRONA) in Burundi, and in 1990 at the hands of the RPF in Rwanda or speak about JRR (Jeunesse Revolutionaire Rwagasore) of Burundi that killed thousands and thousands of innocent people. Similar to the pigeons, people killed under a disguise. To date, there has not been anyone interested in bringing to justice those who started the war in Rwanda in the 1990 that resulted in the death of more than a million people of whom the large majority were Hutus, contrary to public belief. In Rwanda, we can only remind people that when Professors Alan Stam and Cristian Davenport tried to solve this mathematical problem and dared to make their findings public, the two professors were given 24 hours to leave Rwanda and were branded revisionists and genocide deniers. However, Rwanda was not a Banana Republic in the 1990's without official records of births and deaths. Rwanda has been a structured country, therefore, if an analysis is conducted, results will account for Rwandan who died, where deaths occurred, who caused deaths and the causes of deaths. But of course, no one would take time for this endeavour, because, in the end, it would demonstrate that for Kagame's RPF to take power in Rwanda while representing less than 20% of the population, Kagame had to slaughter countless Hutus. Hutus some of whose bones are now mixed with those of Tutsi victims, and are now labelled as Tutsi genocide victims. This practice of mixing of bones is done to simply keep the country in constant state of horror, while bringing in money from malleable Western tourists who come to see this morbid spectacle of bones and leave with a burning urge to hurt the Hutus branded as being responsible for such loss of human lives. This picture of the lies and conspiracy are is one of the tools used in Burundi and in Rwanda.

It should be remembered that by downing President Habyariman's plane, the Kagame's RPF violated the Arusha Peace Accord that gave Tutsis half of the government positions in a power-sharing agreement which was neither fair nor democratic, but to which the Hutus agreed, for the sake of peace. This similar arrangement was made in Burundi. The agreement in Burundi seems remains in effects but it reinforces to the notion that the rules of democracy cannot be applied to Hutus. Also reinforced is lack of justice where an entire people, in the case of Rwanda, was castigated as being responsible for a genocide, creating the conditions that allowed more than 6 million people including a large number of Congolese Hutus to be slaughtered at the hands of the Tutsi led RPF. This horrific action is documented in the UN Mapping Report which is still gathering dust in some basement at the UN headquarters and not providing justice for those affected. Justice for pigeons is hard to obtain.

Trapping Hutus into committing what can be called a genocide became a strategy and was pursued for thirty years by some Tutsi hardliners, going as far as organizing false flag operations against fellow Tutsi during the RPF war, to take over the country, as was admitted by former RPF officers, years after their conquest. The Assassination of President Ndadaye in Burundi and the shooting down of the plane carrying President Habyarimana of Rwanda and Cyprien Ntaryamira of Burundi, are believed to have been part of this strategy to provoke the Hutus into an overreaction that would be recognized as a genocide by the international community. This starategy to provide Tutsi elite behind this nefarious plan to gain a political bludgeon to hit over the head of the Hutus for years, not surprising, it came to pass with President Yoweri Museveni of Uganda boasted about the genius of this plan by saying, "These people (Hutus) are so corrupt, you provoke them a little and they commit genocide."

In addition to these obvious injustices, the International Community chose to look the other way as Kagames Tutsi army slaughtered and oppressed the Hutus for the last 25 years, unconcerned about any consequences, political, judicial or otherwise. Can you imagine what would have happened in Germany if after the Second World War, Allies had put an extremist Jewish Government in charge of Germany and gave them "free rein" to kill and torture as they please? Yet this is what was done in Rwanda and yet, later, after more than 10 million dead, we are still wondering why. The answer may just be as simple, "What westerner wants is right." Practices must be changed to provide equal right for every citizen.

If there is a phenomenon such as collective psyche, the Hutus, especially those from Rwanda exist from a very dark place which, if explained in modern psychological term, would render mute all the horror movies in the history Hollywood. For centuries the country's symbol of power was a drum called Kalinga which was adorned with human body parts (male genitals, eyes, and female breasts) from conquered Hutu kings and Tutsi recalcitrant characters. This drum was worshiped and handed over from King to King. This drum not only symbolized the annihilation and the total subjugation of the Hutu people, but also an ideology that called for the extermination of everyone related to the conquered kings in what was commonly called stamping out the vendetta (guca inzigo). This is the original genocide ideology which the current Rwanda regime managed to force into the Hutu camp by equating any demands by Hutu for equal rights to an attempt to commit genocide. Now if one pauses to ask what kind of person lives with and carries around a drum that is adorned with human body parts as trophies, there is no doubt that one would conclude that such a person would have to be criminally insane in the most extreme sense of the word. For a nation or a people to be governed by families of these types of individuals for centuries, can only mean that in the end, you have a very damaged nation of people.

Rwanda having been governed by horror for centuries explains some of the submissive behaviour that are still found in the Rwandan population among both ethnic groups with the masses obeying the leaders without questioning the actions they are asked to undertake such as killing each other, or even accepting to be killed without putting up any kind of fight. In other words, we have a nation of much damaged people caused by centuries of being governed by horror. Being caused to live with the piles of skeletal remains of those who perished in the 1994 catastrophe is just another form of governance by horror. Jews and the Armenians buried their dead and they still remember the horrors. Rwandans and Africans in general practice bury their dead. Therefore, one has to be criminally insane to think that exposing human skeletal remains of loved ones to the family's day after day is done for other reason than for cementing terror in children and extreme hatred in adults. The fact is, there are more Hutus remains in those so-called memorials than Tutsis remains as it has been revealed by some Tutsi survivors who know factually that most of them did give their loved ones the proper burial they deserved. These types of wounds cannot heal until Rwanda comes to term with all her past in truth and real reconciliation, with the assistance of well-intentioned qualified professionals. Then and only then, the pigeons might be fed also.

Based on all that is known about human relationships and human development, there is really no need for anyone to be treated like a pigeon amongst other human beings. We know for a fact that in societies where people managed to overcome past wounds to build prosperous nations or societies it took tremendous effort to mend the people's hearts through justice, reconciliation and true forgiveness. That is why, the fact that in Rwanda for example, the victor's justice that never punished criminals from the party that started the war which precipitated the country into a four-year descent into hell, resulting in genocides, war crimes and crimes against humanity, such justice remains one of the main reasons why Rwandans are still trapped in the past that is characterized by horror, waiting for true justice. When you add the horrible and insane practice of not burying the dead, deny mainly Hutus the right to remember their loved ones without being a label of being a criminals, or unfortunate victims of retaliatory acts from aggrieved soldiers or being called acceptable collateral damage from a legitimate liberation war, you have the an emotional quicksand that keeps swallowing any positive impulses to overcome the past. Additionally, you also have constant fuelling source for the active violent volcano that manifests itself into these cycles of violence for which no remedy if found.

The idea of a truth and reconciliation commission for Rwanda should be explored and fully implemented by all those who are sincerely seeking peace and stability in the Great Lakes Region. This must be coupled with an all-encompassing justice system that enthrones the undeniable sacred nature of all human lives so that we never, ever, refer to a group of human beings as pigeons. Those who might be quick to think that advocating for the plight of the Hutus as a persecuted majority in the Great Lakes region implies denying the suffering and the persecution the Tutsis may have suffered as a minority in some parts of the region should consider facts. The fact that one and only way a minority group manages to control larger majority is through extreme violence and manipulation and these actions have the tendency to end with misery and suffering for those associated or identified as being part of the usually, small cliques undertaking this brutal task of minority domination of the majority.

In Burundi, since 1965, some Hutu became refugees and could not return to their home country. In 1972, a million Hutu joined those in exile after 200-300 000 were cruelly slaughtered. In 1988 another significant number of Hutu intellectual escaped the butcher regime in Burundi and ran away. In 1993, instead of running away they decided to build resistance which became CNDD-FDD the ruling party today.

In 2015, it was a mistake to have believed a president from that political party could be overthrown from the expression of street opinion. The action resulted in another flux of refugees to countries in the region, Tutsi in majority and few Hutu from FNL obedience who were fuelled by false prophetic rumours of mass killing following an eventual assassination of the actual President of the Republic of Burundi.

All this created wonderingly groups of young people, trained militarily with few fire guns on the top of the refugees reported by the UNCHR. The phenomenon is alarming and needs high attention. Those forces can, anytime, be used to destabilise the region of the Great Lakes of Africa. The root of evil of Burundi is not a third term mandate or the personality of the actual president of Burundi as it is presented by most opinion. The problem of the country is the unfinished business of all those years, the deep wounds of the nation of Burundi and the lack of justice.

The root of the evil of the nation of Burundi are conspiracy and traps established by few western manipulators. They fuel conflicts by injecting hate and finance into minority groups causing cyclical wars that take human lives and leave many who are wounded, orphans and widows. Based on atrocities in the nation of Burundi since 1962, many people of Burundi present with symptoms of exposure to war. Symptoms associated with trauma, disaster, abuse and neglect presenting in persons exposed to war and in children born to parents who were exposed to war.

Research show that long-term consequences of a child exposed to traumatic events, abuse or neglect are similar what is seen in Burundi communities. Such as:

- Intergenerational transmission of abuse and neglect is a reality in the country. (Although most survivors of child maltreatment do not go on to maltreat their own children, some evidence suggests that adults who were abused or neglected as children are at increased risk of intergenerational abuse or neglect compared to those who were not maltreated as children (Kwong, Bartholomew, Henderson, & Trinke, 2003; Mouzos & Makkai, 2004; Pears & Capaldi, 2001). In a study by Pears and Capaldi (2001), parents who had experienced physical abuse in childhood were significantly more likely to engage in abusive behaviours toward their own children or children in their care. Oliver (1993);

-Considering the cycle of violence, there is undoubtedly re-victimisation in the country. (Research suggests that adults, particularly women, who were victimised as children are at risk of re-victimisation in later life (Cannon, Bonomi, Anderson, Rivara, & Thompson 2010; Mouzos & Makkai, 2004; Whiting, Simmons, Havens, Smith, & Oka, 2009; Widom, Czaja, & Dutton, 2008)

-While statistical data from studying the health problems cause by abuse and neglect in Burundi is lacking, observation shows that, the country has many people with health problems and there is a high rate of mortality. Parallel inference can be made from other nations experiencing negative health effects from abuse and neglect. Example is seen in, (Adults with a history of child abuse and neglect are more likely than the general population to experience physical health problems including diabetes, gastrointestinal problems, arthritis, headaches, gynaecological problems, stroke, hepatitis and heart disease (Felitti et al., 1998; Sachs-Ericsson,

Cromer, Hernandez, & Kendall-Tackett, 2009; Springer, Sheridan, Kuo, & Carnes, 2007).

- Although the culture and structures of the family in Burundi plays a major role in resilience, it is very common to find people who exhibit mental health problems in the country. (Persisting mental health problems are a common consequence of child abuse and neglect in adults. Mental health problems associated with past histories of child abuse and neglect include personality disorders, post-traumatic stress disorder, dissociative disorders, depression, anxiety disorders and psychosis (Afifi, Boman, Fleisher, & Sareen, 2009; Cannon et al., 2010; Chapman et al., 2004; Clark, Caldwell, Power, & Stansfeld, 2010; Maniglio; 2012; McQueen, Itzin, Kennedy, Sinason, & Maxted, 2009; Norman et al., 2012; Springer et al., 2007)

- Suicidal behaviors are throughout the country. Considering the multiplicity of rebel groups of the country, suicidal behaviour are attributable to the ill effects of abuse and neglect resulting from practices of rebel groups. (Consistent evidence shows associations between child abuse and neglect and risks of attempted suicide in young people and adults (Felitti et al., 1998; Gilbert et al., 2009; Norman et al., 2012). In the Adverse Childhood Experiences (ACE) study in the United States, Felitti et al. (1998) indicated that adults exposed to four or more adverse experiences in childhood were 12 times more likely to have attempted suicide than those who had no adverse experiences in childhood. In a meta-analysis by Gilbert et al. (2009)

- Eating disorders and obesity cannot be attributed to overeating from abundance. The state of poverty in the country simply precludes overeating from abundance (Eating disorders and obesity are common among adult survivors of child abuse and neglect (Johnson, Cohen, Kasen, & Brook, 2002; Kendall-Tackett, 2002; Rodriguez-Srednicki & Twaite, 2006; Rohde et al., 2008; Thomas, Hypponen, & Power, 2008). Prospective research studies have consistently shown links between child abuse and neglect and obesity in adulthood (Gilbert et al., 2009)

- In Burundi, alcohol and substance abuse are common and have become tolerable ways of dealing with the stress of living in constant reminder of past harrows. (Associations have often been made between childhood abuse and neglect and later substance abuse in adulthood (Gilbert et al., 2009; Simpson & Miller, 2002; Widom, White, Czaja, & Marmorstein, 2007). In a systematic review of 224 studies, a strong relationship was found between child physical and sexual abuse and substance abuse problems in women (Simpson & Miller, 2002). Less of an association was found among men, although men with child sexual abuse histories were found to be at greater risk of substance abuse problems. The authors suggested that it is possible that men are less likely to disclose childhood abuse due to social values and expectations (Simpson & Miller, 2002).

-Continuing for years following the 1965 event in Burundi, aggression, violence and criminal behaviour resulted in thousands of victims. (Violence and criminal behaviour are another frequently identified long-term consequence of child abuse and neglect for adult survivors, particularly for those who have experienced physical abuse or witnessed domestic violence (Gilbert et al., 2009; Kwong et al., 2003; Miller-Perrin & Perrin, 2007). Widom (1989)

- Sexual immorality increase is consistent and spreading to unexpected groups and bring increased health risks. Today, even churches are haven of high-risk sexual behaviors. (Adults who have experienced childhood abuse and neglect, particularly child sexual abuse, are more likely to engage in high-risk sexual behaviour. This can lead to a wide range of sexually transmitted diseases or early pregnancy (Cohen et al., 2000; Hillis, Anda, Felitti, Nordenberg, & Marchbanks, 2000; Norman et al., 2012; Steel & Herlitz, 2005; Young, Deardorff, Ozer, & Lahiff, 2011).

- Burundi has many wandering groups of people in wilderness areas of the Great Lakes region in addition to homelessness throughout the country. (Strong associations have been made between histories of child abuse and neglect and experiences of homelessness in adulthood. A study by Herman, Susser, Struening, and Link (1997) found that the combination of lack of care and either physical or sexual abuse during childhood was strongly associated with an elevated risk of adult homelessness. Adults who experienced a combination of a lack of care and either child physical or sexual abuse were 26 times more likely to have been homeless than those with no experiences of abuse. In a study examining whether adverse childhood events were related to negative adult behaviours among homeless adults in the United States, 72% of the sample had experienced one or more adverse childhood events (Tam, Zlotnick, & Robertson, 2003).

Burundi citizens are being exposed to horror. Teaching of hatred, division and evil doing are spread among all ethnic groups. Immoral behaviours are considered as bravery. Insulting a person and seeking to harm by any mean have become common. Killing children or anyone with poison is seen as a normal and decapitate victims after killing them with gun or any other egged-iron is applauded and likened to earning a trophy. Social networks is overflowing with what is called sensational news, such as images of people who are killed, wounded and insulted/bullied. People have grown to enjoy and like more evil than good.

The nation of Burundi is very wounded and needs healing. It carries all the consequences persons who were exposed to war, trauma, disasters, abuse and neglect. International and national commissions have failed because they are just legalistic tools and is clearly not what the nation of Burundi needs the most. The Peace Building Commission, the International Human Commission, the International Criminal Court, even the United Nations Security Council have wrong appreciation of the reality of Burundi because they base their opinions on one- sided rival reports. They are operating similarly to a medical doctor treating his patient with a lethal dose of medicine based on the wrong diagnosis. The National Human Commission, the National Commission Against Genocide, the National Unity Commission as well as the Truth and Reconciliation Commission cannot be effective at all in the actual context of the country. Those commissions are like vases of flowers in a house of horrors. A witchdoctor does not cure himself because sickness needs to be understood from purely technical perspective to be treated. To be peaceful, prosperous and stable, Burundi nation does not need a power sharing agreement of the Arusha, or any kind of Peace Agreement or protocoled ethnic based laws.

The Arusha Peace Agreement was an effective tool to end the civil war that ended following the 1993 killing of the democratically elected president and many members of his government but it is not a fair and authentic solution to the matter of the nation of Burundi. The agreement is biased. Instead of being related to the constitution, it rather reinforces the conscience of ethnic rival by the ethnic quotas.

The healing of wounds of the nation needs mostly the practice of simple defined principles such as:

- A clear establishment of the truth of the past;

- Good governance;

- Equal right and opportunities to all citizens;

- The freedom of expression, speech, religion, assembly and press;

- The Rule of Law, where no one is above the law;

- Right to life and liberty;

-Developing plan that gives hope of a bright future for everyone, citizens and foreign nationals living in Burundi.

1. The Responsibility of the Government of Burundi

Burundi is a member of the United Nations and the African Union. It has ratified a numerous number of international and regional human rights treaties and thus has made binding international commitments to adhere to the standards laid down in these universal human rights documents.

The government of Burundi of 1966-1976 was charged with legislative, judicial and executive duties and had exclusive control including execution and implementation of laws and policies to maintain peace, public order and protect its citizens. To the contrary, the government of Burundi planned and executed extermination policies such as the Simbananiye Plan and other measures against its citizens from Hutu ethnic group.

As an executive institution of the state in Burundi, the government of 1966-1976 was responsible for maintaining law and order in its jurisdiction. However, at least 300 000 Hutu citizens were brutally tortured and killed between 29 April, 1972 and September 1972, while Micombero was in power. The mass killings of Hutus in1972, with public executed so widespread that the horrific events were well known to the then government. Yet, even though such government had powers and authority to prevent the afore-mentioned mass killings of Hutu, the Micombero regime never made attempts such as seeking assistance from the regional or international organizations such as the then OAU, currently African Union (AU), or the United Nations. The government's conduct and omissions proved to be failure of the government to assume its obligations under international law. Thus, in such failure, petitioners allege and submit that the government of 1966-1976 be held criminally responsible for the genocide of 1972 against the Hutus in terms of customary international law.

Genocide is distinct from other crimes inasmuch as it embodies a special intent or dolus specialis. Special intent of a crime is the specific intention, required as a constitutive element of the crime, which demands that the perpetrator clearly seeks to produce the act charged. Thus, the special intent in the crime of genocide lies in "the intent to destroy, in whole or in part, a national, ethnical, racial or religious group, as such".

Thus, the government of Burundi had a special intent to commit genocide and other international crimes against Hutus. A crime of genocide can be inferred to have been committed if the acts listed under Article 2 of the Genocide Convention were committed against a specific target group, such as national, ethnical, racial or religious group. For example, the government's conduct, actions and inactions and its responsibility for genocide and gross violations of human rights in Burundi are evident in the testimonies from the survivors and victims of genocide of 1972 listed above.

On the account of the various testimonies of the ways in which the 1972 mass killings of Hutu were conducted, there are clear indications of a special intent or dolus specialis to commit genocide and other heinous crimes against Hutus in Burundi.

2 Requests and Recommendations

The survivors and victims of 1972 genocide against Hutus in Burundi, along with thousands of other civilians Tutsi and Hutu combined have been the victims of gross violations of international law for more than 42 years. In order to vindicate their rights, to uphold respect for international law, and to deter future human rights abuses, the United Nations Human Rights Council should consider this petition in terms of paragraphs 85, 86 and 87 of the UNHRC Resolution 5/1, and undertake thorough investigations on the systematic grave violations of the human rights committed against Hutus in Burundi. It is important to emphasize that the Genocide Convention affirms that genocide is a crime punishable under international law for which the international community must condemn and hold accountable the perpetrators.

Hence, petition submits that the government of Burundi of 1966-1976 committed the crimes of genocide, direct and public incitement to commit genocide, crimes against humanity, particularly extermination, murder, torture, rape and other inhumane acts against Hutu ethnic group in 1972. Additionally, the Government of Burundi violated the Common Article 3 to the Geneva Conventions, which are all punishable under Article 4 of the Genocide Convention.

Taking into account the facts, the petition requests and recommends that:

1.   The United Nations Human Rights Commission mandates a diligent investigation into the mass atrocities committed by the Micombero government against Hutus with the view to map out the extent of the massacres and ascribe criminal responsibility to the perpetrators.

2.   The 1972 Genocide against Hutus be recognized under international law once the investigations have confirmed the reality and the extent of the atrocity committed with the intent to wipe out all Hutu intellectuals.

3.   Prosecute and punish the perpetrators whose criminal responsibility will have been established through an appropriate judicial investigation.

4.   Burundi judiciary be transformed, and law reforms be effected in pursuit of a fairer justice system taking into account the pernicious effect of impunity on the social harmony of the country.

5.   Establish without delays a Truth and Reconciliation Commission and Special Criminal Tribunal pursuant to the Arusha Peace and Reconciliation Agreement, 2000 and UN Security Council Resolution 1606 of 2005

6.   Reparations for the victims of the 1972 genocide against Hutus which must include governmental public apology, have national heritage sites such as construction

of a permanent exhibition showing photos, documents and other displays of survivors' experiences

7.   Establish a public holiday of remembrance of 1972 Genocide and other committed atrocities against Hutus.

8.   Establish rehabilitation centres for the survivors and victims of genocide, where citizen will receive collective therapies.

9. Introduce courses on the 1972 Genocide and other atrocities committed in Burundi, into primary schools, secondary schools and university studies.

10. Name selected avenues, roads and hills after victims of the 1972 genocide, promote songs, dances and other cultural tools that inform and educate about the 1972 and other atrocities.

11. Western personalities with negative political influences to be removed from influencing Burundi and Great Lakes region.

Let us all together advocate for the wounded nation of Burundi. Let us make that country a land that flows of milk and honey, peace and prosperity. Let us all together fight for the nation of Burundi while not forgetting Rwanda. As previously stated, the nation of Burundi needs a "Moses"," Joshua" and an "Aaron", and you can be one of them to assist in ways to mend and heal the broken heart before it is too late. This time not mended with lies, conspiracy and cursed human blood, but with love, truth and true reconciliation.-

www.ingramcontent.com/pod-product-compliance
Lightning Source LLC
Chambersburg PA
CBHW081718250726
48657CB00010B/3038